SNIPING IN FR

Sniping in France provides a detailed and richly informative account of how the snipers of the Great War British army trained and fought, and measures taken against their German counterparts. The author was responsible for organising a cohesive structure to the training of the snipers via the First Army School of Scouting, Observation and Sniping, established in 1916.

Written in a very readable style, filled with anecdotes and fascinating detail, the author's study covers the genesis of sniping in the army, his early days instructing XI Corps, and then First Army, including much on the curriculum and work at that unit's School of Scouting, Observation and Sniping. It also includes anecdotal chapters describing sniping memories, before concluding with recollections of training the Portugese Expeditionary Force's snipers, and looking ahead to the future of sniping. Detailed appendices reproduce relevant excerpts from the army's wartime training manuals.

Originally published in 1920, copies are highly sought-after. Helion's reprint is a high quality edition, newly typeset, and featuring a number of charming pencil sketches by Ernest Blaikley.

H. Hesketh-Prichard

The Sniper-Observer-Scout (from a drawing by Ernest Blaikley)

SNIPING IN FRANCE 1914–18

With Notes on the Scientific Training of Scouts, Observers, and Snipers

Major H Hesketh-Prichard
D.S.O., M.C.

With a foreword
by
General Lord Horne of Stirkoke
G.C.B., K.C.M.G., etc.

Helion & Company

Helion & Company Limited
26 Willow Road
Solihull
West Midlands
B91 1UE
England
Tel. 0121 705 3393
Fax 0121 711 4075
Email: info@helion.co.uk
Website: http://www.helion.co.uk

Published by Helion & Company Limited 2004

Designed and typeset by Helion & Company Ltd, Solihull, West Midlands
Cover designed by Bookcraft Limited, Stroud, Gloucestershire
Printed by Cpod, a division of The Cromwell Press Group, Trowbridge, Wiltshire

Originally published by Hutchinson, London 1920
This newly-typeset edition © Helion & Company Limited 2004
This paperback reprint 2009

ISBN 978-1-906033-49-1

British Library Cataloguing-in-Publication Data.
A catalogue record for this book is available from the British Library.

Illustrations by Ernest Blaikley, Artists' Rifles, late Sergeant-Instructor at the First Army
School of S.O.S., and the late Lieut. B. Head, The Hertfordshire Reg., and from Photographs

For details of other military history titles published by Helion & Company contact the above
address, or visit our website: http://www.helion.co.uk.

We always welcome receiving book proposals from prospective authors.

Contents

Foreword

By General Lord Horne, G.C.B.

It may fairly be claimed that when hostilities ceased on November 11th, 1918, we had outplayed Germany at all points of the game.

Perhaps as a nation we failed in imagination. Possibly Germany was more quick to initiate new methods of warfare or to adapt her existing methods to meet prevailing conditions. Certainly we were slow to adopt, indeed, our souls abhorred, anything unsportsmanlike.s

Had it been left to us, "Gas" would have taken no part in the Great European War.

But, however lacking in imagination, however slow to realize the importance of novel methods, once we were convinced of their necessity, once we decided to adopt them, we managed by a combination of brains and energy, pluck and endurance, not only to make up the lost ground, but to take the lead in the race. In proof of this statement I would instance Heavy Field Artillery, High Explosives, Gas, Work in the Air, etc, and many other points I could mention in which Germany started ahead of us, including Sniping, Observation and Scouting.

And for our eventual superiority we owe much to individuals, men who, like the author of this book, Major Hesketh-Prichard, combined expert knowledge with untiring energy, men who would not be denied and could not recognize defeat.

In the early days of 1915, in command of the 2nd Division, I well remember the ever-increasing activity of the German sniper and the annoyance of our officers and men in the trenches. I can recall the acquisition by the Guards' Brigade, then in the Brickfields of Cuinchy with Lord Cavan as Brigadier, of two rifles fitted with telescopic sights and the good use made of them. It was the experience of 1915 that impressed upon us the necessity of fighting for superiority in all branches of trench warfare, amongst which sniping held an important position. It was therefore a great satisfaction to me upon my arrival from the battlefields of the Somme in the autumn of 1916 to find Major Hesketh-Prichard's School firmly established in the First Army area, thanks in a great measure to the support and encouragement of Lieutenant-General Sir Richard Haking, the Commander of the Eleventh Corps.

From that time onwards, owing chiefly to the energy, enthusiasm, tact and personality of its Commandant, the influence of the Sniping, Observation and Scouting School spread rapidly throughout the British Forces in. France. Of its ups and downs, of its troubles and its successes, and of its ultimate triumph, Major Hesketh-Prichard tells the tale with modesty typical of the man.

I may be permitted to add my testimony that in each phase of the war, not only in the trenches, but also in the field, we found the value of the trained sniper, observer and scout.

This book is not only a record of a successful system of training, valuable as such to us soldiers, but also will be found to be full of interest to the general reader.

Chapter One

The Genesis of Sniping

R eaders of this book must realize the necessarily very narrow and circumscribed point of view from which it is written. It is simply an account of some memories of sniping, observation and scouting in France and Flanders, and its purpose is to preserve, as far as may be, in some form the work and training of a class of officers and men whose duties became ever more important as the war progressed. It is in the hope that the true value of sniping and scouting will continue to be recognized in the future training of our armies, as it certainly was recognized in the later years of the war, that this book is written.

The idea of organized sniping was not a new one to me when I went out to France in May, 1915. I had been there before, in the previous March, and had seen the immense advantages which had accrued to the Germans through their superiority in trench warfare sniping.

It is difficult now to give the exact figures of our losses. Suffice it to say that in early 1915 we lost eighteen men in a single battalion in a single day to enemy snipers. Now if each battalion in the line killed by sniping a single German in the day, the numbers would mount up. If any one cares to do a mathematical sum, and to work out the number of battalions we had in the line, they will be surprised at the figures, and when they multiply these figures by thirty and look at the month's losses, they will find that in a war of attrition the sniper on this count alone justifies his existence and wipes out large numbers of the enemy.

But it is not only by the casualties that one can judge the value of sniping. If your trench is dominated by enemy snipers, life in it is really a very hard thing, and *morale* must inevitably suffer. In many parts of the line all through France and Belgium the enemy, who were organized at a much earlier period than we, certainly did dominate us. Each regiment and most soldiers who have been to France will remember some particular spot where they will say the German sniping was more deadly than elsewhere, but the truth of the matter is that in the middle of 1915 we were undergoing almost everywhere a severe gruelling, to say the least of it.

When I went out in May, 1915, I took with me several telescopic-sighted rifles, which were either my own property or borrowed from friends. I was at the time attached to the Intelligence Department as an officer in charge of war correspondents, and my work gave me ample opportunity to visit all parts of the line. Whenever I went to the line I took with me, if it was possible, a telescopic-sighted rifle, and I found that both brigades and battalions were soon applying to me to lend these rifles. In this way opportunities arose of visiting the line and studying the sniping problem on the spot.

One day I remember I was going through the trenches in company with the Australian Correspondent, Mr Gullett, when we came to a very smart notice board on which was painted the word "Sniper", and also an arrow pointing to the lair in which he lay. The sniper, however, was not in the lair, but was shooting over the top of the parapet with a telescopic-sighted rifle. These rifles were coming out from England at that time in very small numbers, and were being issued to the troops.

I had for many years possessed telescope-sighted rifles, and had some understanding of their manipulation as used in big game shooting. In a general way I could not help thinking that they were unsportsmanlike, as they made shooting so very easy, but for shooting at rabbits with a small-bore rifle, where you only wounded your rabbit unless you hit him in the head, they were admirable and saved a great deal of unnecessary suffering.

But to return to the sniper. Much interested, we asked him how he liked his rifle, and he announced that he could put a shot through the loophole of the iron shields in the German trenches "every time." As the German trenches were six hundred yards away, it seemed to me that the sniper was optimistic, and we asked him if he would let us see him shoot. I had with me a Ross glass which I always carried in the trenches, and when the sniper shot I saw his bullet strike some six feet to the left of the plate at which he was aiming. He, however, was convinced from the sound that it had gone clean through the loophole! He had another shot, and again struck well to the left. I had a look at his sight, which was a tap-over fitting, and seeing that it was a little out of alignment I questioned the sniper as to how much he knew about his weapon. It is no exaggeration to say that his knowledge was limited.

From this moment all telescope-sighted rifles became a matter of great interest to me, and it was not long before I came to the conclusion that about 80 per cent were quite useless, much worse, in fact, than the ordinary open sights, in the hands in which they were. The men using them had in most cases hardly any knowledge of how their sights were aligned. A tap or a knock and the rifle was straightway out of shooting.

For the benefit of the untechnical reader it will be well here to remark that if a telescopic-sight set upon a four inch base is one hundredth of an inch out of its true alignment, it will shoot incorrectly to the extent of nine inches at 100 yards, and, of course, 18 inches at 200 yards, and 54 inches at 600 yards. The sights had been issued without instruction, were often handed over as trenchstores, and were served out by quartermaster-sergeants who very often looked on them as egregious fads.

It seemed to me that here was something definite to go upon towards that organization of sniping in which I so much desired to have a hand. That evening I laid the matter before my Commanding Officer, Lieutenant-Colonel A G Stuart, of the 40th Pathans, than whom surely no finer officer went to the war. He was killed in 1916 by a chance bullet a mile behind the trenches, when he was serving near Ypres as GSO1 to the 50th Division.

He listened with both sympathy and interest. "You say, " said he, "that all or nearly all the telescope-sighted rifles you have seen are so incorrect as to be worse than useless. Are you quite sure of this?" "Quite sure," said I. "And that is only one side of it. The men have no idea of concealment, and many of them are easy targets to the Hun snipers."

"The proper authorities should move in the matter," said Colonel Stuart.

"There don't seem to be any proper authorities, sir. The officers know no more than the men about these sights, and what I want to do is this: If it is possible I should like to be appointed as sniping expert to some unit. I believe I could save hundreds of lives even in a brigade the way things are."

Colonel Stuart said nothing, so I went on:

"Will you help me to get a job of this kind, sir? I am asking because it seems absurd for a fellow like me who has spent years after big game to let men go on being killed when I know perfectly well that I can stop it."

"Are you sure of that?"

"I am quite willing, sir, to go to any unit for a fortnight's trial, and if I do not make good, there will be no harm done."

"Well," said Colonel Stuart at length, "we will talk to people about it and see what they say."

After that, Colonel Stuart often questioned me, and I pointed out to him our continued and heavy losses, the complete German superiority, the necessity not only of a course of training but, more important still, the selection of the right men to train and also their value to Intelligence if provided with telescopes, and made a dozen other suggestions, all very far-reaching.

When I look back now on these suggestions, which came from a very amateur soldier of no military experience, I can only marvel at Colonel Stuart's patience; but he was not only patient, he was also most helpful and sympathetic. Without him this very necessary reform might, and probably would, have been strangled at birth, or would have only come into the Army, if it had come at all, at a much later time.

Colonel Stuart not only allowed me to speak of my ideas to various officers in high command, but even did so himself on my behalf. I was amazed at the invariable kindness and courtesy that I met on every hand. I used to introduce myself and say: "Sir, I hope you will forgive me if I speak about a thing I am awfully keen on – sniping, sir. The Huns got twelve of the Blankshires in this Division on their last tour of duty, and I think we could easily beat them at this if we had proper training and organization." And then I would lay out my plans.

But, though people listened, there were immense difficulties in the way, and these might never have been surmounted, although quite a number of Corps and Divisional GOC's had said to me: "If you can get away from your job at GHQ, come here and be our sniping expert. We shall be very glad to have you."

Still, as I say, there is a thing in the Army called "Establishment," and there was no Establishment for a sniping officer, and if the matter were put through the War Office it would probably take some months, I knew, to obtain an establishment. Colonel Stuart, however, once I had convinced him, backed me up in every possible way, going to see the MGGS, Third Army, Major-General Sir A L Lynden-Bell, who was in full sympathy with the idea. It was thus that the matter was mentioned to Sir Charles Monro, commanding the Third Army, and Colonel Stuart arranged with Brigadier-General MacDonogh, now Lieutenant-General Sir George MacDonogh, who was then in command of the Intelligence Corps, to allow me to serve with the Third Army as sniping expert.

John Buchan, who was at that time the *Times* correspondent on the Western Front, also gave the idea great encouragement. He had seen for himself the awful casualties that we were suffering, and considered the scheme which I laid out to be a sound one.

Sir Charles Monro, in talking over the matter, made a remark which I have always remembered.

"It is not" he said, "only that a good shot strengthens his unit, but he adds to its *morale* – he raises the *morale* of his comrades – it raises the *morale* of the whole unit to know that it contains several first-class shots."

These are not the exact words which Sir Charles used, but they are as near them as I can remember.

Now that I had got my chance I was at first extremely happy, but later, as I could not go to my new work at once, I became a little nervous of failure, and pictured myself unsuccessful in my attempt to dominate the German snipers. I began to wish that I had gone to my work a month earlier, for when the Third Army took over from the French, the Germans offered any amount of targets, whereas I now heard that they were becoming more cautious. I, therefore, cast about for some way in which I might hope to make certain of success, and to this end, having conceived a plan, I went down to Neuve Chapelle, where my friend, Captain A C Gathorne-Hardy, 9th Scottish Rifles, since killed at Loos leading his men and within ten yards of the German wire, was in the line. We obtained from the old German trenches a number of the large steel plates from behind which the German snipers were wont to shoot, and these I took home with me to England, for I had obtained a week's leave before taking up my new duties.

I proceeded to try on these plates all kinds of rifles, from the Jeffreys high velocity .333 to heavy elephant guns of various bores, and was delighted to find that the bullets from the .333, as well as the elephant guns, pierced them like butter. Here, again, Colonel John Buchan came to my assistance, and obtained for me a fund, to which Lord Haldane, Lord Glenconner and Lord Finlay kindly contributed the money, and which enabled me to purchase the necessary rifles. Later on, Mr St Loe Strachey, the editor of *The Spectator*, continued to keep up my fund, which really was of incalculable value to us, and out of which everything from dummy heads purchased at Clarkson's to football jerseys for the splendidly appointed Sniping School, which finally eventuated, were purchased.

At length I was free of my work at GHQ, and went down to the Third Army, where I was attached to the 7th Corps, the 4th Division, and the 10th and 12th Infantry Brigades.

It would be out of place to describe in detail the days that followed. Suffice it to say that very early in the proceedings it became clear that snipers must always work in pairs, one man shooting and one man finding the targets with the telescope. The regulation issue of the latter was at the time, I think, about eight telescopes per battalion, and these were used by the Signalers, but Lord Roberts' Fund, administered with extraordinary energy by Mr Penoyre, came to the rescue, and soon a certain number of telescopes dribbled down into the 4th Division line. As to the heavy and armour-piercing rifles, they did their work exceedingly well, and no doubt caused a great surprise to the enemy.

One day I obtained leave to go to Amiens, where I visited the French Camouflage Works, and found to my delight that they had made a number of *papier-mâché* models of the heads and shoulders of British soldiers. Of these I was able to purchase a large quantity, and had no longer any need to buy in London, where the heads were rather theatrical properties than the real thing. The uses to which the heads were put were varied. They were, in these early days before they were too much advertised (for they afterwards became an issue in our Army), most useful in getting the enemy to give a target. It was also possible, by showing very skillfully the heads of Sikhs or Gurkhas in different parts of the line, to give the German Intelligence the impression that we were holding our line with Indian troops, and I have no doubt they were considerably worried to account for these movements.

One day I received orders from Army Headquarters telling me that Colonel Langford Lloyd, DSO, had now started a telescopic sight school in the 10th Corps area, and ordering me to go there and to collaborate with Colonel Lloyd in a book upon sniping and telescopic sights. I went and found a splendid school running, in which the instruction in telescopic sights was rapidly correcting these rifles in the 10th Corps.

I had the opportunity at Colonel Lloyd's school of learning a great deal that I did not know about telescopic sights and many other matters in which Colonel Lloyd is a past master. He listened with great interest to the various ruses, of which there was now quite a long list, that we had employed in the trenches.

We wrote our pamphlet on sniping and telescopic sights, a pamphlet which, owing to a change in the Army Command, was never published, and shortly after my visit to Colonel Lloyd I received the intimation that my trial time with the Third Army had been successful, and that steps would now be taken to get me placed permanently upon its strength. In the meantime, I went from brigade to brigade, burning with eagerness to make organized sniping a definite fact. The instruction took place both in and out of the trenches, and during the course of it we had many interesting experiences. As soon as people began to talk about sniping as a new and interesting subject, our arrival in the trenches became rather trying, as we were certainly looked upon as something in the light of performing animals who would give some kind of a show of greater or less interest. But the Higher Command soon put a stop to this, and thenceforward we were allowed to plough our lonely furrow.

It would be difficult to describe the various days spent in the trenches, or the duels that took place there; but each one threw fresh light upon sniping and showed the enormous extent to which it might be developed. I will make some reference to these days in later chapters.

As I have stated, snipers always worked in pairs, one observing, the other shooting, and soon we found that the notes kept by the observer were invaluable from an Intelligence point of view. If a line was well covered with snipers' posts, nothing could happen in the enemy line without our snipers' observers reporting it – no work could be done, no alteration in the parapet made. Successful observation was, in my experience, first obtained in the 10th Brigade, commanded by Brigadier-General Hull, by the 2nd Seaforth Highlanders. They had an extraordinarily keen Commanding Officer, who provided his men with good telescopes.

We now began all through the 7th Corps to start sniping sections consisting of trained snipers and observers, and the success of the movement grew very rapidly. The German began to cower in his trenches, and as time wore on our casualties grew less and less. My life at this time was an extraordinarily interesting and strenuous one. Moving from brigade to brigade, I would often find splendid arrangements for testing the telescopic sights, and as often none at all. A horse before breakfast, on which I would set forth to find a range, followed by an hour in the Pioneer's shop, pasting up targets made out of old *Daily Mails* onto frames – the snipers of the brigade paraded at nine o'clock, the march to the improvised range, shooting the telescopic sights at the target, and after dark a lecture in some barn, was often the order of the day.

I think in these early days that I was exceedingly fortunate in having something definite to show. The telescopic sights were often very much out of shooting, and no one understood the cure. I think many thought for the first time that there was something in this sniping movement when a sniper missed the target three times running at 70 yards, and a little later, after his rifle had been manipulated, scored three bulls on end.

One thing that struck me was the extraordinary interest taken by all Brigade Commanders in every detail of the work. I do not say, nor do I think, that at the beginning they looked on my coming with unmixed favour. Once I walked into a Brigade Headquarters, and while waiting in the passage heard a voice say:

"Who is this blighter who is coming?" And then someone gave my name. Then a voice said: "Plays cricket, doesn't he?"

I could not help laughing, but as I say, in the very early days every Brigade Major and GOC had to be converted to a belief in sniping. Often and often the Brigade Commanders would spend hours on the first day at the range, and I think that without exception when they saw the incorrect rifles being made correct, they once and for all decided in my favour. On my second visit to these Brigades, I was almost always made the guest of the Brigadier-General and received with a kindness so great as to be really overwhelming. Things, in fact, were going very well indeed for the work which one hoped would soon spread through the whole BEF, for to my delight one day I received a letter from Major Collins, then GSO2 to the Second Army, whom I had informed of my appointment as sniping expert, to say that General Plumer was starting an Army Sniping School in the Second Army, and asking for any notes I might have.

But one morning while shooting on the range I heard that Sir Charles Monro and his staff had gone to Gallipoli. I had been so keen on my work that I had not pushed the matter of getting my appointment regularized, but now I realized that its tenure might become very insecure. Indeed, as a matter of fact when I did raise the question I was informed by GHQ that if I did not keep quiet I should be recalled.

In 1915, the Third Army was far and away the best sniping Army in France. There was hardly an incorrect sight in the 10th or 7th Corps, and scores of officers and hundreds of men had been through courses at Colonel Lloyd's 10th Corps School, or with me. It was while I was with one of the Infantry Brigades of the 37th Division that I received a letter which gave me immense pleasure. It was to the effect that Lieutenant-General Haking, the Corps Commander of the 11th Corps in the First Army, wished to borrow me, so that I might lecture on sniping to his Corps and go through their telescopic sights. Here was a splendid chance of carrying the work outside my own Army.

About this time I was attached to the Third Army Infantry School, then just formed under its first and very capable Commandant, Brigadier-General R J Kentish, DSO. I lectured there on sniping and started a range and demonstrations, but I found myself lecturing to Company Commanders, whereas I ought to have been doing so to sniping officers, in order to get the best results. The Company Commanders liked, or appeared to like, the lectures, but, in the Army phrase, it was "not their pidgin," and I soon felt that I should do better work nearer the line.

From the school, however, I journeyed up into the First Army area, and went through the sights and fulfilled my engagement with the 11th Corps. I think these days as the guest of the various Corps Commanders of the First Army – for I was passed on from the 11th Corps to the 3rd, and from the 3rd to the 1st – were the best days I had in France, for the extraordinary keenness in the First Army was very marked. It was here that I had to go through the ordeal of having to lecture to the Guards Divisional Staff and Snipers at nine o'clock in the morning. In lecturing, even on an interesting subject like sniping, it has always seemed to me much easier to be successful in a warm room at five o'clock rather than in a cold one at nine.

After finishing with the First Army and correcting some 250 telescopic sights, I went back to the Third Army Infantry School. Here I found that the Army Commander of the Third Army, Sir E H H Allenby, had applied for my services for the Third Army, and had received the reply that these could be granted provided I relinquished the staff pay I was receiving and was willing to accept instead the lower rate of an Infantry Captain. This, of course, I agreed to do. Evidently, however, there was some further hitch, for I received no pay for the next eight months, nor did I dare to raise the question lest I should be sent back to GHQ.

I remember one General saying to me upon this question, not without a smile, "You are not here officially, you know, and any Germans you may have killed, or caused to be killed, are, of course, only unofficially dead."

I will conclude this chapter with a letter that I wrote in November, 1915, which gives my impressions at that date.

MY DEAR—

Since I have been with the 3rd Army, I have had an Officer from every battalion in the 7th Corps through my course. These Officers in their turn train snipers, and so the thing permeates quickly and, I think, with really good results.

Sniping seems to me to be the art of–

I. Finding your mark.

II. Defining your mark.

III. Hitting your mark.

With regard to No 1, it is absolutely essential that the use of the telescope should be taught from the stalking or big game point of view. If we had one Officer teaching it in every battalion of our Army in France, we should kill a lot of Germans, and not only this but the task of Intelligence Officers would be greatly facilitated. With four good telescopes on every battalion front, very little can happen in the enemy line without our knowing it. There are a good many telescopes in France.

With regard to defining a mark. It is here that telescope sights help us, but telescope sights in the hands of a man who does not thoroughly understand them are utterly useless. I have had a great many through my hands, and in every ten I have had to correct about six after they have been in the trenches a short time. I wish every battalion had an Officer who could correct and shoot telescopic sights. It is very important that he should be thoroughly knowledgeable, because a rifle barrel must not have too many shots fired through it. With a new barrel a good shot can nearly always get a three-inch group, but after 600 or 1000 shots have been fired through the barrel the group becomes more scattered. It is therefore necessary that the man who regulates the rifle behind the trenches should be able to do so with as few shots as possible.

Another point is, that men must be trained to understand and believe in their telescopic sighted rifles. One Brigade I had for instruction, on the third day of instruction with 16 snipers shooting, got 17 hits on a model of a human head at 430 yards in the first 21 shots. Some of the rifles used by these men had been six or eight inches off at 100 yards until regulated. In all they got 27 hits in 48 shots on the head, shoulder hits not counted.

Also I have been having Officers through a regular course. I give them first of all 20 objects, such as models of heads of French, British and German soldiers, periscopes, rifle barrel, pickaxe, fire lighted, etc. These objects are shown for fifteen seconds each from a trench, and those under instruction have to write a list of what they can see with a telescope from 600 or 700 yards away. It is wonderful how quickly they come on. After a short time they can spot the colour of the pieces of earth thrown up from the trench under observation. Then I give them a hillside to examine. On this hillside I place a couple of objects which are easy to find, perhaps the heads of a Frenchman and an Englishman. I also put in two carefully concealed loopholes, which they usually fail to find. This teaches thoroughness of search.

The construction of loopholes is most important. In this we are behind the Germans. There is one form of double loophole, which I am keen to see more universally adopted. The plate is placed in the parapet, and two feet behind it a second plate is placed in grooves along which it will slide. Not once in a hundred times does the German at whom one is shooting get his bullet through both loopholes.

The drainpipe loophole is also very good. If put in at an angle, it is very difficult for a German to put a bullet down it. In fact if the drainpipe is put in low in the parapet, the brave Hun has to come clean over the top of his own parapet to shoot down it at all.

I am also keen on teaching our fellows to open loopholes sanely. I usually lie in front watching, and it is rarely that, if I shot straight, I should not be able to kill or wound nine of every ten men who open them. Loopholes should, of course, be opened from the side, and a cap badge exposed before they are looked through. If the German does not fire for 75 seconds, one may conclude that it is fairly safe. These little simple-sounding precautions can save so many lives.

I cannot help feeling that sniping, even in these days of many specialists, should be organized and improved. My aim has always been to work in with battalions. Some are better than others, naturally so, but always without exception I have found them very keen on improving sniping.

The use of snipers in attack is another point. If you have a man who can hit a model of a human head once in every 2 shots at 400 yards – and I will undertake to get most men up to this standard who can shoot decently – we shall kill some machine-gunners in our next advance. Also when a German is shooting at our troops coming down a road through an aperture made by the removal of a brick from a wall, as they have often done, how useful to have a fellow who can put a bullet through the aperture.

Of course no telescopic sight should ever be touched, except as far as moving the focusing sleeve goes, by anyone who does not understand it thoroughly. When the object-glass becomes dirty or fogged with wet, snipers often unscrew it. Unless they put it back in its exact original position, they of course alter the shooting of the rifle hopelessly. They also unscrew the capstan heads, which are for the lateral regulation of the sighting. I have seen telescopic sights which were 30 inches out at 100 yards, or about 25 feet at 1000 yards. These things would be impossible under a keen sniping Officer.

One thing I am certain snipers can do. They can make it very hot for the enemy's forward artillery observing Officers. If when the enemy shell our trenches, one can get on the flank, one can often spot a Hun Officer observing. The thing to do then is to lay a telescope on through a drainpipe loophole nearby. If you pack in the rifle on to a bed of sandbags so that the pointer of the telescopic sight rests just *under* the place where the Hun pops up, it is possible to take aim and fire the rifle in from two to four seconds. It is very important that the man who is to shoot should look through the big telescope and get a map of the trench opposite into his brain. Our telescopic sights magnify about 3½ and one can often make a successful shot by shooting six inches or a foot left or right, or above or below a white stone or some prominent object in the opposing parapet, even when you cannot define the Hun's head very clearly through the sight.

I have seen this done. It is a very good sign when the Hun's field glasses fall on the wrong side of the parapet.

Another thing to which we might give attention is the use of decoys. I have had some made for me by the French.

I am quite convinced if I were asked to give the Germans the impression that we had been relieved by Sikhs, Gurkhas or Frenchmen, that I could do so, so wonderful are the models made for me by the French sculptor. It is impossible to tell them from the real thing if skilfully exposed at 100 yards, unless the light is very strong, and at 300 and 400 yards it is quite impossible.

In fact as long as trench warfare lasts, I believe much can be done in many small ways, if desired. But 1200 or 1500 telescopic sights in the hands of trained men and four times as many optical sights, *if full value is got out of them*, might along our line shorten the German Army of many a valuable unit before the spring.

Again and again battalions report two, three or four Germans shot by their snipers in a single day; if you reduce these claims by half or even if each battalion snipes but one Hun a day – and this is an absurdly low estimate where adventitious sights are skilfully used, the loss to the Germans would be great.

I have received the most kindly welcome possible from everybody, and in many cases, almost in all, the Corps have been asked to let me go back to give further instruction. All Brigadiers are very keen indeed to get a high standard of sniping, and many of them feel that to do this is almost impossible unless the snipers are trained to their rifles until their belief in their own powers of hitting a mark, however small, becomes fixed.

As I think of sniping all day and often dream about it at night, I could write you a lot more on the subject, of which I have only touched the fringes. If we organize sniping, we can get solid and tangible results by killing the enemy and *saving the lives of our own men*. Only those who have been in a trench opposite Hun snipers that had the mastery know what a hell life can be made under these conditions.

I don't think the Germans are better snipers than our men, except that they are more patient and better organized and better equipped. I have found out a good deal about the German sniping organization, but this is too long to go into now. I have said nothing of piercing and blowing in German plates with heavy and .333 rifles. You can shut up their sniping very promptly for a time in this way.

Chapter Two

The Sniper in the Trenches

I

In my last chapter I attempted to give some history of the small beginnings of organized sniping, and I will now turn to the actual work of sniping in the line.

Sniping, which is to be defined in a broad way as the art of very accurate shooting from concealment or in the open, did not exist as an organized thing at the beginning of the war. The wonderful rapid fire which was the glory of the original expeditionary force was not sniping, nor was it, beyond a certain degree, accurate. Its aim was to create a "beaten zone" through which nothing living could pass; and this business was not best served by very accurate individual shooting. Rather it was served by rapid fire under skilled fire-control. But when we settled down to trench warfare, and the most skilful might spend a month in the trenches without ever seeing, except perhaps at dawn, the whole of a German, and when during the day one got but a glimpse or two of the troglodytic enemy, there arose this need for very accurate shooting. The mark was often but a head or half a face, or a loophole behind which lurked a German sniper, and no sighting shot was possible because it "put down the target." The smallest of big game animals did not present so small a mark as the German head, so that sniping became the highest and most difficult of all forms of rifle shooting. At it, every good target shot, though always useful, was not necessarily successful, for speed was only less necessary than accuracy, and no sniper could be considered worthy of the name who could not get off his shot within two seconds of sighting his target.

So much for the sniper in trench warfare, of which a certain clique in the Army held him to be the product. The officers who believed this prophesied that when warfare became once more open he would be useless. This proved perhaps one of the most short-sighted views of the whole war, for when it became our turn to attack, the sniper's duties only broadened out. Should a battalion take a trench, it was the duty of snipers to lie out in front and keep down the German heads during the consolidation of their newly-won position by our men, and were we held up by a machine-gun in advance, it was often the duty of a couple of snipers to crawl forward and, if possible, deal with the obstruction.

I am here, however, going ahead of my narrative, but I want early in this book to state definitely that the sniper is not, and from the first, as I saw him, *never was meant to be, a product of trench warfare.* In modern war, where a battalion may be held up by a machine-gun, it is invaluable to have in that battalion a number of picked shots who can knock that machine-gun out. For this purpose in some of our later attacks a sniper carried armour-piercing ammunition and did not shoot at the machine-gunners but at the machine-gun itself. A single hit on the casing of the breech-block, and the machine-gun was rendered useless.

In the Army there has always been in certain quarters a prejudice against very accurate shooting, a prejudice which is quite understandable when one considers the aims and ends of musketry. While sniping is the opportunism of the rifle, musketry is its routine. It would obviously never do to diminish the depth of your beaten zone by excess of accuracy. But this war, which, whatever may be said to the contrary – and much was said to the contrary – was largely a war of specialists, changed many things, and among them the accurate shot or sniper was destined to prove his extraordinary value.

But a great deal that I have said in the foregoing paragraphs only became clear later, and at the moment of which I am writing, September and October, 1915, the superiority lay with the Germans, and the one problem was to defeat them at a game which they had themselves started. For it was the Germans, and not the British, who began sniping.

That the Germans were ready for a sniping campaign is clear enough, for at the end of 1914 there were already 20,000 telescopic sights in the German Army, and their snipers had been trained to use them. To make any accurate estimate of how many victims the Hun snipers claimed at this period is naturally impossible, but the blow which they struck for their side was a heavy one, and many of our finest soldiers met their deaths at their hands. In the struggle which followed there was perhaps something more human and more personal than in the work of the gunner or the infantryman. The British or Colonial sniper was pitted against the Bavarian or the Prussian, and all along the front duels were fought between men who usually saw no more of their antagonists than a cap badge or a forehead, but who became personalities to each other, with names and individualities.

Only the man who actually was a sniper in the trenches in 1915 can know how hard the German was to overcome. At the end of 1914 there were, as I have said, 20,000 telescopic sights in the German Army, and the Duke of Ratibor did good work for the Fatherland when he collected all the sporting rifles in Germany (and there were thousands of them) and sent them to the Western front, which was already well equipped with the military issue. Armed with these, the German snipers were able to make wonderfully fine shooting. Against them, lacking as we did a proper issue of telescopic sighted rifles, we had to pit only the blunt open sights of the service rifle, except here and there where the deer stalkers of Scotland (who possessed such weapons) lent their Mannlichers and their Mausers. But for these there was no great supply of ammunition, and many had to be returned to their cases for this reason.

At this time the skill of the German sniper had become a byword, and in the early days of trench warfare brave German riflemen used to lie out between the lines, sending their bullets through the head of any officer or man who dared to look over our parapet. These Germans, who were often Forest Guards, and sometimes Battle Police, did their business with a skill and a gallantry which must be very freely acknowledged. From the ruined house or the field of decaying roots, sometimes resting their rifles on the bodies of the dead, they sent forth a plague of head wounds into the British lines. Their marks were small, but when they hit they usually killed their man, and the hardiest soldier turned sick when he saw the effect of the pointed German bullet, which was apt to keyhole so that the little hole in the forehead where it entered often became a huge tear, the size of a man's fist, on the other side of the stricken man's head. That occasional snipers on the Hun side reversed their bullets, thus making them into dum-dums, is incontrovertible, be-

The Sniper's End (from a drawing by Ernest Blaikley)

cause we were continually capturing clips of such bullets, but it must also be remembered that many bullets keyholed which were not so reversed. Throughout the war I saw thousands of our snipers' bullets, and I never saw one which had been filed away or otherwise treated with a view to its expanding upon impact.

At that time in the German Army there was a system of roving snipers; that is, a sniper was given a certain stretch of trench to patrol, usually about half-mile, and it was the duty of sentries along his beat to find and point out targets for him. This information I got from a prisoner whom I examined soon after I went down to the trenches. Indeed, I used to go any distance to get the chance of examining a prisoner and so learn something of the German organization. One deserter gave quite a lot of information. He had the Iron Cross and was a sergeant. One of the scenes that always remains with me is the examination of this man on a rainy, foggy night by the light of a flaring smoky lamp in the room of an *estaminet* just behind the lines. As time went on it became very difficult for a German prisoner to lead me astray with wrong information. There were so many questions to which one got to know the answers, and which must be more or less common knowledge to German riflemen. The demeanour of prisoners was very diverse. Some would give no answers – brave fellows these, whom we respected; others would volunteer a good deal of false statement; others yet again were so eager to answer all questions that when they did not know they made a guess. But one way and another, through them all I gained an immense amount of information as to the German sniping organization.

It would appear that the telescopic-sighted rifles in the German army were served out in the ratio of six per company, and that these rifles were issued not to the private soldiers who shot with them, but to NCOs who were responsible for their accuracy, and from whom the actual privates who used the rifles obtained them, handing them back at given intervals for inspection. In the top of the case of each German telescopic sight were quite short and very clear instructions, a very different matter to the conditions obtaining upon our side, where very often, as I have before stated, the man using the telescopic sight knew nothing about it.

On one occasion I had gone down on duty to a certain stretch of trench and there found a puzzled looking private, with a beautiful new rifle fitted with an Evans telescopic sight.

"That is a nice sight," said I. "Yes sir."

I examined the elevating drum, and saw that it was set for one hundred yards. "Look here," I said, "you have got the sight set for a hundred. The Hun trenches are four hundred yards away."

The private looked puzzled.

"Have you ever shot with that rifle?," I asked. "No, sir."

"Do you understand it?" "No, sir."

"How did you get it?"

"It was issued to me as trench stores, sir." "Who by?"

"The Quartermaster Sergeant, sir."

Certainly many a German owed his life in those earlier days to the fact that so many of the telescopic sighted rifles in the British Expeditionary Force were incorrectly sighted to the hold of the men using them. By this I mean that some men hold tightly and some men hold loosely, and there may be a difference at a

Examination of a German Prisoner (from a drawing by Ernest Blaikley)

hundred yards of six inches in the shooting of the same rifle in different hands. To hand over the rifle as "trench stores," in which case it would be shot by different men of different battalions, was simply to do away with the accuracy which formed its only asset.

But to return to the examination of German prisoners. One point cropped up over and over again, and this was the ease with which German snipers quite frankly owned that they were able to distinguish between our officers and men in an attack, because, as one said naïvely: "the legs of the officers are thinner than the legs of the men." There are hundreds and hundreds of our officers lying dead in France and Flanders whose death was solely due to the cut of their riding breeches. It is no use wearing a Tommy's tunic and a webbing belt, if the tell-tale riding trousers are not replaced by more commonplace garments.

In 1915 there were very few loopholes in the British trenches, whereas the Germans had a magnificent system. In early days when I used to be told at Brigade Headquarters that there was a German sniper at such and such a map reference, and I was to go and try to put him out of action, I very rarely found a loophole from which I could reconnoitre him. As every German sniper seemed to be supported on either flank by other German snipers, looking for him with one's head over the top of the parapet was, if made a continual practice, simply a form of suicide. I used, therefore, to have a couple of sandbags filled with stones and rubble placed as inconspicuously as possible on the top of the parapet. No ball will pierce a sandbag full of stones, and it was thus that one got the opportunity of a good look at the German trenches without fear of receiving a bullet from either flank.

At this time the efforts to camouflage our loopholes were extraordinarily primitive – indeed, concealment was nearly impossible in the form of parapet then in use. Many of our units took an actual pride in having an absolutely flat and even parapet, which gave the Germans every opportunity of spotting the smallest movement. The parapets were made of sandbags beaten down with spades, and it is not too much to say that along many of them a mouse could not move without being observed by the most moderate-sighted German sniper. It was curious how some few commanding officers stuck to these flat parapets in the face of all casualties and the dictates of common-sense, even after the High Command had issued orders upon the subject. At a later date a trial was instituted, and proved that in spotting and shooting at a dummy head exposed for two and four seconds over a flat parapet, the number of hits was three to one, as compared with the same exposure when made over an imitation German parapet.

Over on the other side of No Man's Land the German trenches presented a quite different appearance from ours – ours being beaten down, as I have said, until they made as clear a line as a breakwater. The German trenches were deeper, with much more wire in front, and from our point of view looked like the course of a gigantic mole which had flung up uneven heaps of earth. Here and there, a huge piece of corrugated iron would be flung upon the parapet, and pinned there with a stake. Here and there stood one of those steel boxes, more or less well concealed under a heap of earth, from which set rifles fired all night. Here and there lay great piles of sandbags, black, red, green, striped, blue, dazzling our eyes. It was said that the Germans used the pink and red ones to look round, because they approximated to flesh colour, but this was no doubt apocryphal. But what was not apocryphal was the fact that the Germans had a splendid parapet behind which a man could move and over which he could look with comparative impunity, whereas we in this respect gave heavy hostages to fortune.

There was one protection which was always sound, and which could be put into immediate operation, and that was to teach our men to hang as many rags as possible upon our wire and wherever else they could in the region of our parapet. These fluttering rags continually caught the German eyes, which were drawn by the movement of the rags in the wind. It is possible that, if the truth were recognized, those simple little rags saved many a life during the course of the war. Of course, there were battalions in which attempts had been made to remedy these defects, as there was one type of officer whom one occasionally came across. This was the soldier who had done a certain amount of stalking, or big-game shooting, and it is not too much to say that wherever there was such an officer, there were usually two or three extra telescopes and telescopic-sighted rifles, and various well concealed posts from which to use them. The Intelligence report, which was each day forwarded to Brigade, was also full and accurate. Indeed, the truth of the matter forced itself upon me, as I spent day after day in the trenches. *What was wanted, apart from organization, was neither more nor less than the hunter spirit.* The hunter spends his life in trying to outwit some difficult quarry, and the step between war and hunting is but a very small one. It is inconceivable that a skilled hunter in a position of command should ever allow his men to suffer as our men sometimes did in France. It was all so simple and so obvious. The Canadian Division and, later, the Canadian Corps was full of officers who understood how to deal with the German sniper, and early in the war there were Canadian snipers who were told off to this duty, and some of them were extraordinarily successful. Corporal, afterwards Lieutenant, Christie, of the PPCLI, was one of the individual pioneers of sniping. He had spent his life hunting in the Yukon, and he simply turned the same qualities which had brought him within the range of the mountain sheep to the downfall of Fritz the Forest Guard.

In the long monotony of the trenches during that bleak winter of 1915 the only respite besides work which was possible to our soldiers was the element of sport and excitement introduced by sniping and its more important and elder sister, observation. Sniping in a dangerous sector – and there were many of these – was really neither more nor less than a very high class form of big game shooting, in which the quarry shot back. As to danger, there are in Africa the lion, the elephant, the buffalo and the rhinoceros. Though the consensus of instructed opinion agrees that in proportion more hunters come back feet foremost from lion hunting than from the pursuit of the three other forms of dangerous game, yet I suppose that no one would dispute that the German sniper, especially when he is supported on either flank by *Kameraden*, was far more dangerous in the long run than any lion.

In sniping, as the movement grew and sections were formed, one relied to an enormous extent upon the skill of the section to which the individual sniper belonged. A really first-rate man in a bad section was thrown away. First-rate men under a moderate officer were thrown away, and, worse than all, a good section under a good officer, who were relieved by the slack and poor section of another battalion, often suffered heavy casualties through no fault of their own.

Thus, the Royal Blankshires, who have an excellent sniping organization, build half-a-dozen skilfully hidden posts for observation and sniping purposes. All kinds of precautions, which have become second nature, are taken to prevent these posts being given away to the enemy. The telescopes used are carefully wrapped in sandbags, their sunshades carefully extended lest the sun should, by flashing its reflection upon the object glass, give away the position. The loopholes in dry weather are damped before being fired through, and, most important of all, no one but the CO, the sniping officer, and the snipers and observers are allowed in the posts. If anyone else enters them there are for him heavy penalties, which are always enforced. The result is that the Blankshires have a good tour of duty, lose no casualties to enemy snipers, and get splendid detail for their Intelligence reports.

They are relieved, however, by the Loamshires. The CO of this battalion does not believe very much in sniping. He has a way of saying that sniping will "never win the war." He has, it is true, a sniping section because, and only because, his Brigadier and his Divisional General are keen about sniping, and continually come into the trenches and inquire about it. But the Loamshire sniping section is a pitiable affair. They take over from the Royal Blanks.

"These are jolly good observation posts," says the Royal Blanks sniping officer. He is the real thing, and he dreams of his job in the night. "But one has to be a bit careful not to give them away. I never let my fellows use the one in Sap F until the sun has worked round behind us."

"Aw-right oh!" says the Loamshire opposite number.

"One has to be a bit careful about the curtains at the back of those loopholes in Perrier Alley. The light's apt to shine through."

"Aw-right oh!" says the Loamshire officer.

"We are leaving our range-cards."

"Aw-right oh!"

So the keen Royal Blanks officer and his keen section go out into rest billets, and do not visit the trenches again till they come back to take over from the Loamshires.

"Well, how are the posts?" asks the Royal Blanks officer, cheerily.

"Pretty rotten; they were all busted up the first day."

"Damn! They took us a fortnight to build."

"Well, they are busted up all right."

"Did your fellows give them away, do you think?"

"Oh, no!"

Now, as a matter of fact, the moment the Royal Blankshires were out of the trenches the Loamshire snipers, who knew no better, had used the OPs for promiscuous firing, and the posts which had been so jealously guarded under the Blankshire regime had been invaded by Loamshire officers and men in need of a view of the German trenches – or of sleep. The curtains that kept the loopholes dark had been turned back. The result was as might have been expected. The watching German, who had suffered from those posts without being able to locate them when the Blankshires were in the trenches, now spotted them, rang up their guns, and had them demolished, not without casualties to the Loamshires. So the work was all to be done again – but no sooner does the keen Blankshire officer

Outside the Snipers' Post. "Shut the loopholes. I'm coming in." (from a drawing by Ernest Blaikley)

build up a post than the slack Loamshire officer allows it to be given away. It is now a case for the Royal Blanks CO to take up with the Loamshire CO.

Such were the difficulties of the keen officer when the opposite number of the relieving battalion was a "dud."

Conscientiousness is a great quality in an officer, but in the Sniping, Scouting and Observation Officer something more was needed. To obtain success, real success, it was necessary that his should be a labour of love. He must think and dream of his work at all hours and all times, and it was wonderful how many came to do this. In the battalion the Intelligence and Sniping officer had always a sporting job, and if he suffered in promotion (as do nearly all specialists in any great Army) yet he had the compensations which come to an artist in love with his work.

There were at this time one or two other factors in the situation to which I must allude in order that the reader may understand the position as it was then. The enemy had an immense preponderance in trench weapons such as *minenwerfer*. The result was that a too successful bout of British sniping sometimes drew a bombardment. The activity of snipers was therefore not always welcome to short-sighted officers, who distinctly and naturally objected to the enemy riflemen calling in the assistance of the parapet-destroying engines of war, in which they so outclassed us.

Soon, however, it was realized that the state of things obtaining while the German held the mastery of aimed rifle-fire could not be permitted to continue – the casualties were too great – and I will now give some account of the instruction and experience in the trenches that went on while we were attempting to capture the sniping initiative from the enemy.

II

Towards the end of October, 1915, I was ordered to report to the 48th Division, then holding a line in the neighbourhood of Hebuterne. I was to proceed to Divisional Headquarters behind Pas, and was there ordered to Authie, where a number of officers were to come for instruction. This instruction was, as usual, to be divided between the back areas and the front line. I had applied for the services of my friend, Lieutenant G M Gathorne-Hardy, an experienced shot, and skilled user of the telescope, who had been many shooting trips in different parts of the world with me and others. At Authie we at once settled down to work, the officers going through a course which need not be detailed here. Suffice it to say that the telescopic sighted rifles of all the battalions in the Division were shot and corrected, and various plans which we had formed for the destruction of German snipers were rehearsed.

On the third day arrangements were made by Division as to which trenches we were to visit, and after duly reporting at Brigade Headquarters in a dug-out in Hebuterne, we proceeded upon our way.

It is not an easy thing to instruct five or six officers in the line in sniping – the number is too large – so as soon as we entered the trenches I divided my class into three parties, and assigned to each an area in which to look for German snipers, Gathorne-Hardy and I going from one group to another.

At the point at which we entered the front line trenches, our line was a little higher than that of the enemy, so that the initial advantage was certainly with us,

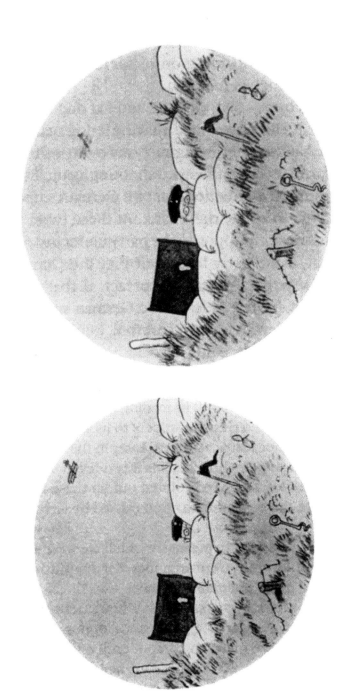

Telescopic Sights. "Nurse Your Target."
1 "Not Yet."
2 "Now!"

and almost at once G (for so I shall refer to Captain Gathorne-Hardy) spotted a German sniper who was just showing the top of his cap at the end of a sap. He was about three hundred and fifty or four hundred yards away, and though we watched him for half-an-hour, he gave no target. So we moved on. Examining the enemy line was enthralling work, as he had, even at that time, begun his campaign of skilled concealment, and was apt to set periscopes in trees and steel boxes in all sorts of positions.

To spot and actually place these upon the map was as important a duty of the sniper as killing the enemy by rifle fire. For, once discovered, such strong points and emplacements could be dealt with by our artillery.

But to return. G and I, after visiting the sections, acted together as shooter and observer. After spending a couple of hours examining the enemy line, we got into a disused trench and crawled back to a little bit of high ground from which we were able to overlook a group of poplar trees which grew between the lines, and which were said to be the haunt of a very capable German sniper.

Nothing, however, was to be seen of him, though we could clearly make out the nest he had built in one of the trees and, on the ground, what appeared to be either a dead man lying in the long grass or a tunic.

While we were here a message came down to say that No 1 group had seen a party of nine Germans, and had wounded one of them. No 2 party had not been successful.

At the time of which I write the Germans were just beginning to be a little shy of our snipers on those fronts to which organization had penetrated, and it was clear that the time would arrive when careful Hans and conscientious Fritz would become very troglodytic, as indeed they did. We had, therefore, turned our minds to think out plans and ruses by which the enemy might be persuaded to give us a target. We had noticed the extraordinary instinct of the German Officer to move to a flank, and thinking something might be made out of this, we collected all our officers and went back to the place where G and I had spotted the Hun sniper or sentry at the end of the sap. A glance showed that he was still there.

I then explained my plan, which was that I should shoot at this sentry and in doing so, deliberately give away my position and rather act the tenderfoot, in the hope that some German officer would take a hand in the game and attempt to read me a lesson in tactics.

On either flank about 150 yards or so down the trench I placed the officers under instruction with telescopes and telescopic sighted rifles, explaining to them that the enemy snipers would very possibly make an attempt to shoot at me from about opposite them. I then scattered a lot of dust in the loophole from which I intended to fire, and used a large .350 Mauser, which gave a good flash and smoke. As the sentry in the sap was showing an inch or two of his forehead as well as the peak of his cap, I had a very careful shot at him which G, who was spotting for me with the glass, said went about twelve inches too high.

The sentry, of course, disappeared, and I at once poured in the whole magazine at a loophole plate, making it ring again, and by the dust and smoke handsomely giving away my own position. I waited a few minutes, and then commenced shooting again. Evidently my first essay had attracted attention, for two German snipers at once began firing at me from the right flank. At these two I fired back; they were almost exactly opposite the party under instruction, and it was clear that, if the party held their fire, the Germans would probably give fine targets. As a matter of fact, all that we hoped for actually happened, for the exasperated German snipers, thinking they had to deal only with a very great fool, began to fire over the parapet, their operations being directed by an officer with an immense pair of field-glasses. At the psychological moment, my officers opened fire, the large field-glasses dropped on the *wrong* side of the parapet, as the officer was shot through the head, and the snipers, who had increased to five or six, disappeared with complete suddenness. Nor did the enemy fire another shot.

It should be borne in mind, in reading the above, how great a plague were the skilled German snipers to us. One of them might easily cause thirty or forty casualties. Later in the war we had, on our side, many a sniper who killed his fifty or even his hundred of the enemy. Besides, as I have pointed out, in these early days of trench warfare the continual attrition caused by German snipers was very bad for *morale*.

At a later date we found a means by which we were able at once to find the position of any German sniper. For this purpose we used a dummy head made of *papier-mâché*.

The method of using was as follows: When a German sniper was giving trouble, we selected a good place opposite to him, and drove two stakes into our own parapet until only about a foot of them remained uncovered. To these we nailed a board on which was fashioned a groove which exactly fitted the stick or handle attached to the dummy head. This stick was inserted in the groove and the dummy head slowly pushed up above our parapet. If the enemy sniper fired at and hit the head, the entry and exit of the bullet made two holes, one in the front and one in the back of the hollow dummy head.

The head, immediately on the shot, was pulled down by whoever was working it in as natural a manner as possible. The stick on which it was mounted was then replaced in the groove, but *exactly the height between the two glasses of a periscope lower* than the position in which it was when shot through.

Now all that remained to do was to place the lower glass of the periscope opposite the front hole in the head, and apply the eye to the rear hole and look into the periscope, the upper glass of which was above the parapet.

In this way we found ourselves looking along the path of the bullet, *only in the opposite direction to that in which it had come*, and, in the optical centre of the two holes, would be seen the German sniper who had fired the shot, or the post which concealed him.

Once found, he was soon dealt with.

In trials at First Army Sniping School, we were able by this invention to locate sixty-seven snipers out of seventy-one.

Some of those who wanted to give the dummy head a specially life-like appearance, placed a cigarette in its mouth, and smoked it through a rubber tube.

It is a curious sensation to have the head through which you are smoking a cigarette suddenly shot with a Mauser bullet, but it is one that several snipers have experienced.

After the incidents last described, we went up towards the flank, where the 4th Division lay alongside the 48th. It was in this Division that the 2nd Seaforth High-

Spotting the Enemy Sniper (from a drawing by Ernest Blaikley)

landers had just played a delightful trick on the enemy. Someone in the battalion had obtained a mechanical stop, one of those ticking bits of mechanism which are made with a view to saving the employment of a human "stop" at covert-shoots. This particular stop was guaranteed to tick loudly for hours.

The Seaforths were facing the Germans across a very wild piece of No Man's Land. One night some adventurous and humorous spirit crawled out and placed the "stop" about sixty yards from the German parapet, and then set it going. The Germans at once leaped to the conclusion that the tick-tick-tick was the voice of some infernal machine, which would, in due time, explode and demolish them. They threw bombs, and fired flares, and officers and men spent a most haggard and horrible night, while opposite them the Scotsmen were laughing sardonically in their trenches. The whole incident was intensely typical of the careless and grim humour with which the Scottish regiments were at times apt to regard the Hun.

Another battalion at a much later date, when the Germans had become very shy, and mostly spent their off-duty hours in deep dug-outs, had the brilliant idea of preparing a notice board on which was printed in large letters and German: "Bitter Fighting in Berlin," and then, in smaller type, some apocryphal information. This notice it was their plan to raise, having first posted their snipers, who would be sure to obtain shots at the Huns who attempted to read the smaller lettering with their field-glasses. I do not think, however, that this plan was ever actually carried out. This was fortunate, since, though ingenious, the idea was not sound, as it would inevitably have led to a heavy bombardment of the trenches in which the notice was shown, and the game would not have been worth the candle.

To continue, however, with our day. Late in the afternoon, no Germans having shown themselves since the shooting of the officer, a heavy bombardment broke out on the right flank. We hurried in that direction, as experience had taught me that the German Forward Observation Officers often did their spotting for the guns from the front-line trench on the flank of the bombarded area.

Sure enough, we soon picked up one of those large dark artillery periscopes, shaped like an armadillo. It was being operated by two men, as far as could be seen. One of them wore a very high peaked cap, and was at once called "Little Willie;" the other had a black beard. The nearest point to which we could approach was more like five than four hundred yards, and though we waited till dark, Little Willie did not show more than his huge cap peak and an inch or two of forehead. As evening fell, we went out of the trenches without having fired, as soon after our arrival the bombardment had ceased, and Little Willie never gave a. good target, and the bearded man had disappeared. I did not wish to disturb the German FOO's in their post, as, now that they were discovered, arrangements could be made to deal with them when next they were observing.

The opportunity occurred three days later, when, after a very long vigil, an officer shot Little Willie, and the same evening a Howitzer battery wiped out the post for good and all.

As, when Little Willie met his end, he was just in the act of spotting the first shots for his battery, which had opened on our front line trenches, his death probably saved us some casualties, for it temporarily stopped the activities of his guns.

It was not only the number of the enemy that our snipers shot that was so important. It was often the psychological moment at which they shot them that gave their work an extra value.

In the autumn of 1915 there came high winds following frosty nights. It was clear that a heavy fall of the leaf would take place on the following days. I therefore asked, and obtained leave from the 4th Division, to which I was at the time attached, to drop instructional work, and instead to go into the trenches in order to spot enemy snipers and artillery observation officers' posts. On my way down I called at Headquarters, where I was told that a very troublesome sniper was operating at Beaumont Hamel. This man had killed a number of our fellows. He was supposed to live in a pollarded willow, one of a row not very far from Jacob's Ladder, which will be remembered by all who were on that front in 1915. There was on that day a certain amount of mild shelling of the communication trenches, but before the advent of gas-shells this rarely caused trouble in the daytime, except to those who had to repair the breaches. On the day in question I was alone with my batman, who, I can say, without fear of libel, shot better than he "batted," for he had been chosen because he was a marksman. Arrived in the front line, we at once set about trying to locate the sniper. As a rule, in such a case, the enemy one seeks is taking a siesta, but this was not so now, for as soon as I looked over the parapet a bullet, striking low, knocked some dust into my eyes. At this point, you must understand, our trenches were shaped like an arm, with a crooked elbow, the crook or turn of the elbow being at the bottom of a hill. In front lay Beaumont Hamel, where in the German lines when I arrived a soldier had hung out his shirt to dry. Between us and Beaumont Hamel lay a wild piece of No Man's Land, with some dead ground on the Beaumont Hamel side, and at the bottom of the hill the row of willows from which the sniper was supposed to operate.

As these willow trees were out of sight from the place where I had been fired at, I did not put down that shot to the sniper, whom we will call Ernst. In this I was probably wrong, as transpired later.

All that morning we tried to locate Ernst, who had four more shots at me, but all that I had learned at the end of it (when I imagine Ernst went off for a well-earned siesta) was that he was a good shot, as though obviously some distance away, he had made quite good practice. We most carefully examined the pollarded willows, and spotted one or two good snipers' posts, especially one at the bottom of a hedge, but as far as Ernst was concerned he had all the honours.

The next day I was occupied all the morning with an enemy artillery OP which was destroyed by howitzer fire, and it was not till after lunch that I could turn my attention once more to Ernst.

This time I began at the bottom of the hill. There were no loopholes, so it was a case of looking over, and almost at once Ernst put in a very close shot, followed again by a second which was not so good. The first shot had cut the top of the parapet just beside my head, and I noticed that several shots had been fired which had also cut the top of the sandbags. Behind the line of these shots was a group of trees, and as they stood on slightly higher ground I crawled to them, and at once saw something of great interest. In the bole of one of the trees a number of bullets had lodged, all within a small circle. Crouching at the base of the tree, and with my head covered with an old sandbag, I raised it until I could see over the parapet fifty yards in front. I found at once that the line of these shots, and those which had struck the tree behind my head, were very nearly the same, and must have been fired from an area of No Man's Land, behind which it looked as if dead ground existed on the enemy's side, and probably from a large bush which formed the most salient feature of that view.

I then went back to the trenches, and warned all sentries to keep a good lookout on this bush and the vicinity. Very soon one of them reported movement in the bush. With my glass I could see a periscope about three feet above the ground in the bush, which was very thick. Being certain, as the periscope was raised so high, and as it had only just been elevated, that it was held in human hands, I collected half a dozen riflemen and my batman, and giving them the range, and the centre of the bush as a target, ordered them to open fire. On the volley the periscope flew backwards and the activities of Ernst ceased forthwith.

It was this experience of looking along the path of the enemy's bullets that led directly to the invention for spotting enemy snipers, which I have described earlier in this chapter.

No one can deny that Ernst was a gallant fellow, lying out as he did between the lines day after day. Whether he was killed or not who can say, but I should think the odds are that some bullets of the volley found their billet. At any rate, sniping from that quarter ceased.

I have now given enough description of the work and training which was going on at that time in the Third Army in the line. The aim and end of all this work was the formation of sniping sections in each battalion, consisting of sixteen privates with two NCOs under an officer.

I had realized that my whole problem turned upon the officer. If I could succeed in obtaining fifteen or twenty officers who would be simply fanatics in their work, it was perfectly clear that the sniping movement would spread like wildfire throughout the Army. Already we had got together an immense amount of detail concerning the German sniping organization and had begun not only to challenge his superiority, but also to enforce our own. It is wonderful what can be done in a single week by sixteen accurate shots along the length of line held by a battalion. You must understand also that the success of the German sniping rested largely upon the deeds of certain crack snipers, who thoroughly understood their work, and who each one of them caused us heavy casualties. The first work to be done in the trenches was the organized annihilation of these skilled German snipers, and I think this was the easier in that they had it their own way for so long.

As time went on, the reports from the brigades were very good; one Brigadier even going so far as to wire me: "Only one Hun sniper left on my front. Can you lend me your elephant rifle?" In this particular brigade the Brigadier informed me that he had not lost a man through enemy sniping in four months.

Sniping, I think, or let us say the sniping campaign, may be divided into four parts. During the first, the Germans had the mastery. During the second, our first aim was to kill off the more dangerous German snipers and to train our own to become more formidable. The third was when the Germans had fairly gone to ground and would no longer give us a chance. The idea now was to invent various ways in which to induce them to give a target, and the final period came at a much later date, when great battles were being fought, and the work of sniping was beginning to merge into that of scouting, and snipers were being trained in great numbers to deal with the new situations that were arising every day as the Germans altered their tactical plans of defence.

Chapter Three

Early Days with the 11th Corps and First Army

Towards the end of 1915 my services were again borrowed by the First Army, this time to take a class of Sniping and Intelligence officers through the course of sniping and observation which was already in operation in the Third Army, and also to lecture to a GHQ Intelligence Class on the Observation and Intelligence side of sniping – a big subject.

I went up the long road through Doullens, Frevent and St Pol, which I had traversed so many times from the days when it was impassable with French soldiers before the Battle of Loos to the quieter times which had now dawned. During the war one had very few relaxations of any kind. Shooting was forbidden, games were difficult for the unattached Ishmaelite to obtain, and often for long periods it was impossible to get any change of thought. The long drives to all parts of the line held by the British Army, which were part of my work, were, therefore, exceedingly pleasant by contrast. Wherever there was a battle I used to try and get to it at the earliest possible moment, in order to have the opportunity of examining the German trenches, for as time went on sniping became more and more scientific, and the Germans were always starting some new method which had to be countered. One of the most important points was to obtain specimens of each issue of their steel plates, in order to experiment on them with all kinds of bullets.

But to return to the First Army Class. We were allotted a curious range on the outskirts of the town of Bethune, then a thriving community, which had been hardly shelled at all, although well within the battle area. Our rifle firing took place under cover, and each target appeared through a series of holes cut in a number of brick walls which crossed the range at right angles. The noise in the room of the cottage which formed the 200-yards firing-point was deafening, but as the weather was both wet and cold, head-cover had its advantages.

The class which assembled consisted of a picked officer from each Division, twelve in all. Some I lost sight of afterwards, but two, at least, of this class rose to command their battalions, and one was awarded the double DSO, another the MC and Bar, and several more single decorations.

In order that the class might be taught the manipulation of telescopic sights, all the rifles of the lst Corps which were fitted with these sights or with optical sights were sent down, together with the snipers who shot them, in order that the rifles might be tested for accuracy. As at that time there had been no real organization or instruction in the use of adventitious sights in the Corps, it is not to be wondered at that most of these were incorrect. Of the first eighty, fifty-nine were quite valueless until regulated, and we were hard put to it to correct them as party after party arrived.

At length a party of Scottish Rifles came, every one of whose weapons was entirely correct. They were under the command of a young officer who, when the trial of his men's rifles was over, saluted and said to me:

"Will I stay and help you with the other rifles, sir?"

"Do you understand telescopic sights?"

"Yes, sir."

"Have you done much shooting?"

"Yes, sir."

"Won anything?"

"The King's Prize, and the Scottish Open Championship, and the Caledonian Shield, sir."

"What is your name?"

"Gray, sir."

That evening Corps Staff was rung up and Gray was straightway appointed Corps Sniping Officer. Suffice it to say, that in a few weeks the German snipers had been dealt with in a way that must have amazed them.

Later on, Gray's Division moved into the 11th Corps, where I have always thought that sniping on some sectors reached its high-water mark as far as the year 1916 was concerned. Afterwards he became my assistant at the 11th Corps School, and later at the First Army School. He finally proceeded to the USA, with the rank of Major, to spread the light there. In this he was most successful, receiving the thanks of the Divisional General to whose Division he was attached for the extraordinary efficiency of his work. In my experience of sniping officers in France, two are outstanding, and he was one of them. The other was Major O Underhill, 1st KSLI.

Our class on that queer range in Bethune lasted a fortnight and was instrumental in getting me a bout of sick leave; for when, as part of the instruction, we had to make a trench and build into it various posts such as snipers use, we found ourselves working in an extremely noisome atmosphere. As fix as we could make out, the greater part of the town drainage seemed to be at no great distance under the ground in which we had to dig. The result was a bout of trench fever. The time I spent at home was not, however, wasted, as I was able to collect large numbers of telescopes and get the various courses for sniping instruction written down, which was useful, as I was continually receiving applications for a syllabus from units outside the Third Army.

When I returned to France I was again attached to the Third Army, but not to the Infantry School, who had secured the services of Captain Pemberthy during my absence. This very capable officer did splendid work for the Third Army. Instead, I went down the line and resumed my old work of instructing brigades and battalions. I also went to the Indian Cavalry Divisions.

At this time, I remember, volunteers who possessed a knowledge of the fitting of telescopic sights were asked for in the 7th Corps. The result was exceedingly typical. One private, who sent in his name, stated that he was well acquainted with telescopic sights and their fittings, having been for four years employed by Messrs Daniel Fraser of Leith Street Terrace, Edinburgh, the well-known firm of gun and rifle makers, whose work on telescopic sights stands so deservedly high. The staff who unearthed this applicant did not continue to congratulate themselves on having produced exactly the article wanted, when, through a letter to Messrs Fraser, it transpired that, though it was quite true that the man had been employed by them, the position that he had held in the firm was that of errand boy, and that his knowledge of telescopic sights was consequently not one which they felt they could confidently recommend.

During these days I went back to many of the brigades to which I had been attached six months previously. The casualties among snipers had not been very heavy, and we had fairly obtained the upper hand. At this period troops were massing for the Battle of the Somme, in which the Third and Fourth Armies took part. The use of the telescope was now a matter of immense interest, as Intelligence wanted all the facts they could get about the enemy, and consequently instruction in glass-work for battalion and brigade observers became more and more sought after, and I trained many observers for Major-General Hull, GOC 56th Division. Just at this period, however, there was a change in my fortunes, and I was ordered to proceed to the First Army, to the command of which Sir Charles Monro had just succeeded after his wonderful performance in Gallipoli. I therefore left the Third Army area and went by rail to Aire-sur-Lys, in order to report to First Army Headquarters, which was situated in that town.

It would be absurd to deny that I was very glad to be attached to the First Army, where the keenness which I had seen on my visit at Christmas time to the various Corps Commanders was glorious. Arriving at Aire I reported to the Town Major, and was allotted a room in the hotel called "Le Clef d'Or." Here I was eating my dinner when the Town Major came across and wanted to know if an officer of my name was present. He said that a car was waiting outside and that I was to go direct to the Army Commander's chateau to dine and stay the night.

The next day the Army Commander questioned me very closely about sniping and about all that had occurred with regard to it since he had seen me last. He then informed me that I was to be attached to the 11th Corps and that my orders were the same as they had been under him in the Third Army – to make good shots, and as many of them as possible.

The 11th Corps, since my previous visit, had started a sniping school, where they were putting through five officers and twenty men on short courses. The school was situated on the far side of the Forest of Nieppe, near a place called Steenbecque. I was ordered to make this school my headquarters. It was in charge of Lieutenant Forsyth MC of the 6th Black Watch. A more curious and picturesque-looking spot for a school it would be hard to imagine. The headquarters were in a little Flemish farmhouse, kept by an exceedingly close-fisted family, and the range, which had firing points at one, two, three and five hundred yards, was neither more nor less than a long sloping cornfield. A most satisfactory point about the range – which was an excellent one – was that it was within two hundred yards of headquarters, so that after parade hours were over an immense amount of voluntary work was done upon it. It was here that we first began to tend towards the really much longer and more detailed course of instruction which we afterwards amplified to a vastly greater extent at First Army School, as soon as the courses were lengthened to seventeen days' duration.

From the first it may be said that the men and officers who came upon all these courses were extraordinarily keen. They liked sniping, and still more, observation, because they felt that here, at last, in the great impersonal war, was an opportunity for individual skill. The more imaginative of them realized also the enormous possibilities of the trained observer. In other chapters I will give several instances of the observation of small details which have had consequences of the most far-reaching nature. I think that this feeling of the ever-present possibility of the opportunity of being able to do a big thing formed part of the fascination of the SOS courses – SOS in this case meaning, "Sniping, Observation and Scouting," and not "Service of Supply," as it does in the American Army.

It has been said, and truly, that soldiers are pretty destructive, but the fact remains that hundreds of privates, NCOs and officers went through their shooting courses in the Steenbecque cornfield, which was traversed in all directions by narrow paths, and yet it was difficult to find any downtrodden ears of corn. Our one difficulty was that at one of the firing points the corn grew up and obscured the targets. It had, therefore, to be cut to the area of about ten yards. I do not know what the claim sent in by the farmer was for this damage, but as far as claims were concerned nothing was ever missed by the Flemish peasant.

Although it was my Headquarters, I used only to spend the first two days of every course at the school; the other days I passed attached to various divisions and brigades, and in this way became conversant with the trench line of the Corps along the whole length of which I inspected the snipers' posts. The 33rd Division, who were holding the line opposite Violaines and the Brick-stacks, had had a tremendous duel with the German snipers. This line has always been a difficult one from the sniper's point of view, as the Germans had, unfortunately, the best of it as to position. The Brickstacks made ideal sniping-posts, and there were many other points of vantage which were very much in their favour. It shows, however, what a first-class sniping officer can do when it is realized that the 33rd Division who, when they went into the trenches, found the Germans very much in the ascendant, soon reduced them to a more fitting state of mind.

It was here that Gray – the sniping officer in question – had a trying experience. One day while making his tour of duty, an officer told him that there was a sniper who was causing them trouble. Gray asked where he was, and was led without words to the part of our trench opposite which the German sniper was supposed to lie. Gray, being signed to do so by his guide, looked over, only to be saluted at about ten yards' range with a bullet which whizzed by his ear.

"That's him," said the officer delightedly. "I knew he was pretty close. But what am I to do? He shoots if one tries to spot where he is."

"Have you never heard of the sniperscope, you …?" demanded Gray.

"By Jove, the very thing!" cried the officer, and it was not long before the German sniper was reduced to impotence.

But to return to the 11th Corps School. Work there was certainly strenuous. There was nothing to do in the village and nothing to do in Morbecque. The nearest place of relaxation was Hazebrouck, and Hazebrouck was out of bounds. The result was that having an interesting course with plenty of rifle shooting competitions, together with occasional mild cricket and football, officers and men were able to concentrate upon the work in hand, and certainly their shooting improved with amazing quickness.

About this time the 33rd Division moved south, and Lieutenant Gray was attached to the School, where he soon left the impress of his personality and methods.

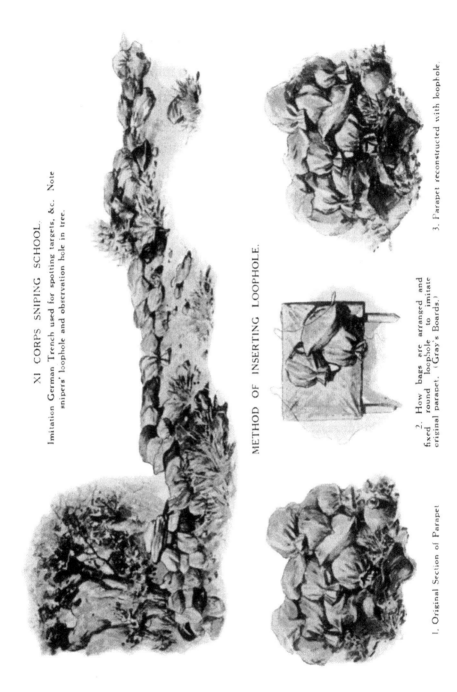

XI CORPS SNIPING SCHOOL.

Imitation German Trench used for spotting targets, &c. Note
snipers' loophole and observation hole in tree.

METHOD OF INSERTING LOOPHOLE.

1. Original Section of Parapet

2. How bags are arranged and
fixed round loophole to imitate
original parapet. (Gray's Boards.)

3. Parapet reconstructed with loophole.

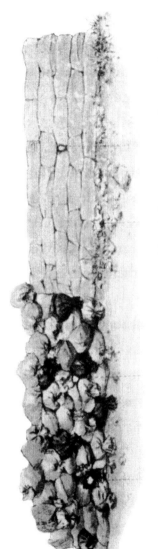

XI Corps Sniping School. Best form of parapet to conceal loopholes. Wrong type of parapet for concealing snipers' loopholes.

Section of typical German parapet. Showing concealed loopholes made through tins, bags, etc. Note – The steel shields on top are dummies.
(Both from drawings by Basil Head)

One of the difficulties that we had always found in the First Army was due to the fact that our trenches, as far at any rate as the Neuve Chapelle-Fauquissart area was concerned, were very shallow, and, indeed we lived rather behind breastworks than in trenches. To make loopholes in these breastworks was exceedingly difficult, but Gray invented a system which we christened "Gray's Boards" which fairly met the case. Thus, if he wished to put in a concealed iron loophole plate, he first of all cut a square of wood of exactly similar size. In this he fashioned a loophole to correspond with the loophole of the iron plate. He then wired the wooden plate on to the iron plate, and having rolled and stuffed a number of sandbags in exact imitation of the parapet in which he wished to insert his loophole, he tacked these with a hammer and tacks upon the wooden board. The whole loophole was then built in at night.

These loopholes of his were rarely discovered, and they had also the added advantage that if a bullet struck them it did not ring upon the iron plate, as it had to pierce the wooden board first, so the posts were never given away by sound.

It was at the 11th Corps School that we first constructed exact imitations of German trenches and German sniping posts; in fact, in one way or another, a great deal of pioneer work was put in there, and the school prospered exceedingly.

The chief reason, I think, for the success of the school was the great personal interest taken in it by the Corps Commander, Sir R Haking, who would come out from his headquarters at Hinges and inspect the school at frequent intervals, as did also Brigadier General W Hastings Anderson, then BGGS of the Corps. We were inspected in July by the Army Commander, and from time to time officers from other theatres of war and from other armies visited us.

In a meadow near the school was a small pond, full of fish, which it was the ambition of Gray and myself to catch. There was only room for two fishermen at a time, and only on one occasion was a fish caught. This we gave to the farmer who owned the pond, and I presume he ate it, for he was up at Headquarters early the next day inquiring for a "*médecin!*"

Still, nothing could be more delightful than after three or four strenuous days, on each of which one walked perhaps eight or ten miles of trenches, to sit before that funny little pool in the French meadow and forget there was a war.

At the time of which I write, the Corps which formed the First Army were the 11th, the 1st and the 4th. The 3rd had gone to the Battle of the Somme. The 1st Corps had a sniping school, which, at a later date, reached an extraordinarily high pitch of efficiency under Captain Crang and the late Lieutenant Toovey, the author of "The Old Drum Major" and well-known Bisley shot. It was a party commanded by Captain Crang which went into the Portuguese trenches, where it was reported the Germans were showing themselves rather freely, and made a big bag. The 4th Corps also had a good school, but they soon moved out of the Army to the south. In fact, when I first went there, the system in the First Army was that which I had always advocated, to have Corps Schools of sniping and observation. The difficulty, of course, was that there was still no establishment, and that sniping schools did not officially exist. This was quite a common thing in the war, for when I first went to the large Third Army Infantry School, with a score of instructors, a large staff, and a couple of hundred NCO and officer pupils, it did not exist officially.

While I was at the 11th Corps School, the War Office at last officially acknowledged my existence as a sniping-officer to the extent that I received my pay, which had been withheld for several months.

After various tours of inspection and work with other Army Corps, I was ordered by the Army Commander to form an Army School of Sniping. Greatly rejoicing, Gray and I borrowed a car from the Army and set out to search through the broad lands of the Pas de Calais. These were delightful days, but search as we would, it was exceedingly difficult to find any place in the area of the First Army which would suit our purpose. It was all too flat. I remember that we once very nearly decided upon a queer little hill, not very far from Hinges, called Mont Bernenchon, but luckily we went on further and at last came to the village of Linghem. Above the village on a high plateau lies an old civilian range backed by a large rifle butt. The plateau on which the range is situated is of considerable extent, and upon its slopes (it was July) bloomed heather and gorse.

"Why," said Gray, "the place is trying hard to be like Scotland!"

The plateau gave us a range of eight hundred yards and plenty of room for playing fields, which the Army always consider to be absolutely necessary to the well-being of a school – one reason, I think, that the health of our men was so good.

Having decided that here was the ideal place for our projected First Army Sniping School, Gray and I were disgusted to see the fresh tracks of a motor car. It was quite clear that somebody else had discovered and had an eye upon our find. We did not even wait for a cup of coffee at the local estaminet but got on board our car and went full speed to Army Headquarters, where we informed the Staff that we had decided upon our location, and were told that as no one else had applied for it, it should be ours. We were only just in time for as we afterwards discovered the Royal Flying Corps had decided to apply for it.

All's well, however, that ends well, and a little later on we left the 11th Corps School with great regret, and set forth on a lorry for Linghem to found the First Army Sniping School.

Often afterwards I used to go across to see how things were getting along at the dear old 11th Corps School. The last time I was there, before it was taken over by a Second Army formation, it was a wintry day with snow falling. I must say that I was glad that I had never been attached there during winter, for what had been a smiling cornfield was now a sea of yellow and glutinous mud. The little *becque* or stream which ran between our stop-butt and our targets had overflowed, and Lieutenant Hands, who had succeeded to the command of the school, was urging some one hundred and fifty odd German prisoners to reconstruct the stop-butt itself. The scene really might have been upon the German "Eastern Front."

Chapter Four

The First Army School of Scouting, Observation and Sniping

The First Army Sniping School was formed for the purpose of training officers, who might act as Instructors in the various Corps Schools, Brigades and Battalions throughout the Army.

The system of Corps Schools was, as I have said, peculiar to the First Army, who, for the next year and a half, turned out three snipers to any other Army's one. Further, the First Army School became recognized throughout the BEF as the training place of observers with the telescope. Indeed, at a later date, we were overwhelmed with applications from Corps and Divisions in other Armies who wished to send observers for a course. This was especially the case before any big movement, and we might almost have guessed where an advance was contemplated by the applications for the training of observers by the units concerned.

However, all this occurred at a later date, and I must pick up my narrative when we left the 11th Corps School in the lorry. Those who were to start the First Army School got aboard after an early breakfast. They were only six in number, Lieutenant Gray, Armourer Staff-Sergeant Carr, Private Fensome (an extremely capable and skilled carpenter), two batmen and myself. We took with us all the spares we could obtain from the 11th Corps School as well as a lot of sniping kit belonging to Gray and myself.

As we rode through the country in the direction of Aire, we passed a huge desolate camp which, I believe, had once been inhabited by Australians. No doubt it had boasted a guard at one time, but it had now fallen into sad disrepair, the Flemish peasantry having appropriated all the stoves and most of the wooden walls. A little further on we came upon two or three Armstrong huts standing in a field adjacent to the deserted camp, and as these were in better preservation, and we had no Armstrong hut of our own, it seemed a pity to leave them for the French, so we set to and took one down and loaded it on the lorry. This was, no doubt, a very wrong thing to do, but when you have no "establishment," you can have no conscience either, or, at least, if you allow yourself such a luxury you will find that your job becomes impossible.

Presently we rolled into Aire over the canal bridge, which was afterwards destroyed by long-range guns, and in Aire we made the little purchases, which are necessary for the formation of officers' and men's messes. We then passed through the old town by the Cathedral. Army Headquarters had moved away, and there was now only the Town Major and one or two ASC columns in possession. On the far side of Aire we took the Lambres and St Hilaire Road, and passed on through the level country. As we turned off through Lambres, we saw, rising in front of us, the high ridge which formed the plateau on which our school was to be situated, and not long afterwards we rode into the village of Linghem. The lorry then went round and disembarked our Armstrong hut upon the plateau, where we at once erected it, and a fortunate thing it was that we did so. That night there were some heavy showers of rain which would have destroyed a good deal of our kit, and more especially our target-paper and dummy heads, had we not put them under proper shelter.

And now, I think, began one of the most interesting periods which I spent in France. Various fatigue men were added to the Staff, and a working party from the Army Service Corps was sent up. We were rather amused to see that the men of this working party, who had been well behind the line for at least a year previously, thought it quite an adventure to come up to the school. When they rolled up their sleeves for digging, we noticed, too, that their arms were white, forming in this a great contrast to our fatigue men. It was necessary to dig trenches, make stop-butts, build snipers' posts and observation posts, and all this hard work the ASC working party tackled with extraordinary energy. We put up goal-posts, and they had a game of football each evening. Several of the ASC party, I believe, were professional football players of repute.

But it would be tedious to describe the growth of the school step by step. Suffice it to say that, beginning with a class of a dozen to fifteen officers, who were dealt with by two officer instructors, our classes grew until we had twenty-five officers and forty or fifty NCOs at each course. But the actual teaching was only one side of the work of the school, for it was soon thoroughly known throughout the Army that if any Division, Brigade or Battalion wanted its telescopic sights tested, or if any individual sniper found himself shooting incorrectly, all that had to be done was to apply to the First Army Sniping School. The divisional snipers came up in busloads, and single snipers often came on foot. This continual testing of rifles kept Armourer Staff Sergeant Carr busy both on the range and in his armourer's shop. Fortunately, as well as being an excellent armourer, Sergeant Carr was also a shot of no mean order, having shot in the King's Hundred at Bisley.

The school had not been long in existence before the Canadian Corps came into the Army. They were then holding the line which they afterwards immortalized opposite the Vimy Ridge, and we were at once struck at the school by their great energy and keenness. There is no doubt that as a sniper, scout or intelligence officer, the Canadian shows the greatest initiative, and during the long period, well over a year, which they remained in the Army, our school was voluntarily visited by two Canadians for every one Britisher. They were most extraordinarily helpful, too, and if ever I wanted the services of some Canadian officer for a particular purpose, they were almost always granted, and not only that, but he was on the spot within a few hours of my application.

At first the greater part of our teaching dealt with sniping, but as time went on the curriculum was much extended. Map reading, intelligence work, the prismatic compass, the range-finder, instruction on crawling, jujitsu and physical drill were all added. In addition to these, we had continual demonstrations of the effect of all kinds of bullets, both British and German, on the armoured steel plates used by us and by the enemy. We formed a museum, which became quite famous, and in which were various exhibits of German and British sniping paraphernalia. We also had many photographs, and again and again officers who had been through the course at the school sent up contributions. It was said that anyone going through

First Army School of S.O.S.

the museum could really gain a very good idea of the development of sniping during the war, and this was by no means an exaggeration.

I soon found that the officers and men who came to the school were really in need of a clear mental change, and this we attempted to provide by giving long hours to games.

For many months the school was "unofficial," but at last, on the 24th November, 1916, more than fifteen months after I had begun serving as a sniping officer, we were granted a "provisional establishment." Up to this time, it was terribly hard to keep the school running, not to speak of the Corps Schools, which were its offshoots. The real difficulty was that when each division moved, all its personnel moved with it. Thus it came about that, seven weeks after the First Army School was started, Lieutenant Gray's division moved out of the Army, and he was recalled to it. In spite of applications from Headquarters that he might be allowed to remain and continue the good work he was doing, this was refused. He went down to the Somme to be made officer in charge of trolleys, or sports, or some such appointment. The mere fact that he was a King's Prizeman and perhaps the best shot and the most capable sniper in the BEF made not one whit of difference. All these qualities are, no doubt, of the highest use in an officer in charge of trolleys!

On Gray's departure, there set in for me a very strenuous time, for at the same moment the Commandant of the 11th Corps School was also spirited away. I found an officer who had been through the course at the First Army School to take his place, and at the same time it became necessary to find a Commandant for the 1st Corps Sniping School. I had at this time no assistant myself, and was dealing with a class of fifteen officers, as well as sometimes as many as fifty snipers, who came up from the line for a day's instruction. My NCOs, however, stepped nobly into the breach, and Armourer Staff Sergeant Carr took over the explanation of telescopic sights – work which lay entirely outside his duties. At that time there were ten or fifteen patterns of these sights in the Army, and each officer on the course had to learn to manipulate every one of them. In fact, the course was a pretty stiff one, and, overworked as I was, it was difficult to be certain how much knowledge the officer students carried away with them, so I started an examination paper on the last day, which was of a very searching nature. The full marks were a hundred, and this paper was continued until the school closed down after the Armistice. Again and again we had classes, the least successful member of which obtained seventy-five of the hundred marks.

During the period in which I was alone after Lieutenant Gray's departure, an officer attended the school who became my assistant, Lieutenant N Hands, of the 11th Warwickshire Regiment. I had great difficulty in obtaining his services, but finally his General exchanged a month of them for some lectures on Sniping by me. As I was taken in a car to and from the lectures – and as they were to be given after parade hours, it did not interfere with my work – this was a very pleasant arrangement, but Hands had not been with me long when there was another upheaval at the 11th Corps School. The 61st Division left, and Lieutenant Benoy, who was in charge of the school, left with it. So Hands went across and took over the 11th Corps School. He afterwards proceeded with the 11th Corps to Italy, where he was awarded the Military Cross and did fine work.

First Army School of S.O.S. No. 1. Flat Parapet. The easiest possible form of parapet to spot movement behind – practically a death-trap.

However, after another period of running the school alone on Hands' departure, Army Headquarters sent me Second Lieutenant Underhill, of the 1st KSL1. Underhill had been wounded at Ypres and came out for instructional duties. The story of his being sent to the school is an amusing one, in the light of after experience, for he was the most tremendous worker that I have ever known. He arrived at Army Headquarters at eight o'clock in the morning, and two hours later, feeling unhappy at still having nothing to do, he went to the GSO1, and asked if he could not be put to work. The GSO1, who was my very good friend, seeing from his papers that Underhill had passed through Hythe, and was stated to be competent as an instructor, sent him out to me. Thus it was that I at last obtained a permanent assistant, and a better no man could have had. Our establishment was still only a tentative one, and it was not until some months later that we were allowed the two extra officers and four extra NCOs, and the dozen scouts and fatigue men, who made up our staff.

Underhill had, by that time, been promoted to Temporary Captain, for good services, and became Adjutant, and Captain Kendall, of the 4th Warwickshire Regiment, who, after a course at the School, had become attached to the Royal Flying Corps as Intelligence Officer, took over the intelligence duties and map reading at the school. Lieutenant W B Curtis, of the 31st Canadian Infantry, became scouting officer. He had had nearly two years' experience between the lines and had been decorated on three occasions.

Our NCOs, too, were the very pick of the Army. There was Armourer-Staff Sergeant Carr, Sergeant Slade, of the Essex Yeomanry, Sergeant Hicks, of the 1st Rifle Brigade, and Sergeant Blaikley, of the Artists' Rifles. All these NCOs became in time amazingly proficient at their work. I have never heard a more clear exposition of the compass than that given by Sergeant Hicks, who, while one squad was firing, would sit down under the bank with the other, and explain to them all the mysteries of the magnetic North.

The physical training of the school was in the hands of Sergeant-Major Betts (Coldstream Guards), one of Colonel Campbell's magnificent gymnastic staff.

Sergeant Blaikley, who had drawn for Punch from time to time, was invaluable as an artist, and it was he who drew our Christmas card – "Der Sportsmann" – depicting a German gassing stags on a Scottish deer forest. This picture, which was very widely circulated, certainly obtained the flattery of imitation, as the same idea was used in most of our comic papers a month or two afterwards.

Captain Kendall was a trained surveyor, and an artist of no ordinary merit. Whatever conundrum was brought up by officers – and a great many were brought up – Kendall, in his own department, was certainly unassailable.

Besides the officers and sergeants, we had another member of the staff who did splendid work. This was Corporal Donald Cameron of the Lovat Scouts. Lord Lovat had visited the school and had expressed his satisfaction at the way in which we were teaching observation and the use of the telescope. I asked him if he could get me a really good stalker to assist me, and he very kindly promised to do so. As one of his own men could not come, he sent me Corporal Cameron, who showed the greatest keenness, and had, I think, a peculiar affection for the last man over the stile. If ever there was a weak member in learning the compass, Cameron would seek him out and explain it. The results were wonderful, and certainly saved several privates from failure.

First Army School of S.O.S. No. 2. Same parapet as in No. 1 after five minutes' alteration. Sandbags have been thrown on top. A man in a sandbag-covered helmet is looking over at A, and a man in a cap is looking between the sandbags at B. Note – Bags must be filled with broken stone or shingle to be bullet-proof, but should be sparsely used in case of bombardment.

Christmas card (1917) of the First Army School of S.O.S. Drawn by Ernest Blaikley.

Cameron, when I asked him his age on his joining, gave it as "offeecially forty-one." He was a very skilful glassman, and as such was of continual assistance to me. I remember one day when we were trying some aspirant reinforcements for Lovat Scouts Sharpshooters and were looking through our glasses at some troops in blue uniforms about six thousand yards away, most of the observers reported them as "troops in blue uniform;" but Cameron pointed out that they were Portuguese. His reasoning was simple. "They must be either Portuguese or French," said he, "and as they are wearing the British steel helmet, they must be Portuguese."

On my establishment, when it finally came along, there were apportioned to me three scouts among the eleven privates to the services of whom the school was entitled. I remember these eleven privates parading for the first time, and I remember also attempting to pick out, with Captain Underhill, the three "Scouts." One of the scouts was a Salvation Army musician, an excellent fellow, but quite unfit for his duties. Another was an ex-barber of the White Star line, and the third had for years been unable to break into a double. As the work of scouts with an Army School is of supreme importance, since one uses them to personate the enemy in scouting schemes, the employment of such men as these was quite impossible. Good fortune here, however, came to our aid, for some performing scouts from GHQ, who were giving demonstrations, came to demonstrate to us, and were afterwards attached to the school. These were boys under nineteen, and the three I kept ended up as past masters of their work. By Armistice Day they had been at the school for some eighteen months, were first-class shots, knew every detail of the course, and could pass an examination equal to any officer. At the physical training and jujitsu, which they had almost every day, they were really young terrors. In fact, I remember a commercial joy-rider who was visiting the school, and whom I was showing round, on seeing two of the boys doing jujitsu, saying with infinite tact: "'Ere, where do you live when you are at 'ome? I'll keep clear o' your street on a dark night."

I might add that all three boys were accomplished Association football players, so that we always had a really first-class centre forward, left wing and halfback upon the premises. Our Association team, for so small a unit, was thus a very strong one, though it might have been much stronger had not so many of the older members of the staff been wounded.

I think the only other member of the staff that I need mention is Sergeant Foster of the Canadians. At a later date, it became our duty to train the Portuguese Army in sniping and shooting, and Sergeant Foster spoke a kind of Portuguese.

I have given at full length this account of the officers and NCOs of the school, because whatever efficiency the school obtained was founded upon their selection. Whenever it was possible to do so, it was always a standing order that between courses, when we sometimes had from two days to a week free, all instructors should go to the line. For this purpose, arrangements were made with different battalions to receive them. This kept the school in touch with the progress of events.

I have often regretted that I did not keep a Visitors' Book at the First Army Sniping School, for certainly enormous numbers of visitors came to us. Outside the officers of the BEF, of whom several hundred visited the school, we had attachés and missions of various allied and neutral powers – Japanese, Rumanian, Dutch, Spanish, American, Italian, Portuguese, Siamese and Polish officers, as well as large numbers of journalists, from whom, when they were not our own accredited correspondents, I used to conceal a good deal of the more secret parts of our work. One day, however, on being informed by the officer-in-charge of the correspondents that they were perfectly safe, and that I could show them anything, I showed them a small new invention by which we were able to spot the position of German snipers. I carefully warned them that it was not to be written about, but about three months later I saw a large and glaring article describing the visit of one of these journalists to the school. The description of the invention could have been of little interest to the great public which he served, but it was there, carefully set out. This was the only case of a definitely-broken promise of this nature which I came across during the war. Our own correspondents, Valentine Williams (afterwards Captain Valentine Williams, MC), Philip Gibbs, Beach Thomas, Perry Robinson, H M Tomlinson, Prevost Battersby, Percival Phillips, and others who came after I left GHQ, were welcome and trusted throughout the whole Army.

The feeling in the Army against the Press – for there certainly was, at one period, such a feeling – is really very often a rather stupid pose adopted by the younger officers, who usually copy some downright senior; but it will always remain as long as journalistic mistakes are made – and that will be as long as wars last.

Outside the members of the staff, we had help from time to time from various officers who were attached for short periods of duty. Among these was Major A Buxton, DSO, of the Essex Yeomanry, who took two classes of Lovat Scouts in observation. He was, I believe, the only officer who was habitually successful in catching trout in the French streams. Second Lieutenant C B Macpherson of Balavil, a true expert with the telescope and map, was also attached to the school for a time. He came out at the age of sixty-two with his splendidly trained group of Lovat Scouts Sharpshooters.

Another officer who was temporarily attached to the staff was Captain T B Barrie of the Canadian Highlanders. He first came to the school on a course, and was afterwards lent to me by the Canadian 4th Division. Shortly after his first visit to the school, he gained two MC's in a fortnight, both in raids, in one of which he penetrated six hundred yards behind the German line. There can have been few more gallant officers in France, and his death later in the war was a matter of deep regret to all who knew him.

One day, Major General the Hon W Lambton, commanding the 4th Division with which I had begun my sniping duties in 1915, came to the school. His division was then in one of the other armies, but he wished to have observers trained, and sent up a party under Lieutenant Kingsley Conan Doyle, of the Hampshire Regiment, the son of Sir Arthur Conan Doyle, and one of the best observation officers we had at any time. Conan Doyle possessed an extraordinary facility for teaching and was most successful with one or two classes of Lovat Scouts, which he took. He went back to his Division, was promoted to Captain, and acted in charge of the Divisional Battle Observers in the big battles of 1917. It is tragic to think that when the order came out for all medical students to return to complete their studies, Captain Conan Doyle went back to England; there he contracted influenza and died. This has always seemed to me one of the saddest things in the war – to have gone through so much, to have rendered such good service, and finally to be struck down by the horrible influenza germ instead of the German shells among which he had walked about so unconcernedly.

I have now given you a somewhat rambling account of the formation, and of those who were chiefly connected with the early days, of the First Army Sniping School. On the very day on which it was founded, Sir Charles Monro left France to take up his appointment as Commander-in-Chief of the Forces in India. Sir Richard Haking succeeded to the temporary command of the Army, and as it happened was the very first visitor who ever came to First Army School. He told us that the King was coming almost at once into the Army area, and that he wished Gray and myself to go back to the 11th Corps School to prepare for a Royal Inspection. This we did, but unfortunately the King was held up in Bethune by shelling, so that there was no time for him to visit us. We greatly regretted this, as a Royal visit would have been of enormous value to sniping at that time.

One visitor who came to the school was of peculiar interest to me. This was my old friend Sir Arthur Pearson, who arrived accompanied by his son, whom I had last seen at the Boys' Cricket classes at Lord's when he was first in the running for the Eton Eleven, of which he was afterwards Captain. He was now an officer in the RHA. Sir Arthur Pearson went over the whole school and asked me many questions. Though he could not, of course, see the loopholes and all the rather technical work, which I explained to him, it was perfectly amazing to realize the way in which he gripped it in its essentials. I think that he knew more about sniping, scouting and observation after the hour or two he spent at the school than I have known other men gather in a week.

First Army School of S.O.S. Sniper's Robe on a 6ft. 4in. man in the open, Hawkins position. Distance from camera, 8 yards.

The only ladies who visited us were Mrs Humphry Ward and her daughter. It was terrible weather when they came, and the little path, which led up to the range, and which was really more or less the bed of a stream, had become a glacier of ice several feet in thickness. On the range the wind was blowing exceedingly cold, and few worse days could have been picked for a visit. I remember Mrs Ward saying to me that she thought sniping – the terrible and ruthless killing of men with weapons of precision – one of the most dreadful sides of the war. I pointed out to her the life-saving side of sniping, and how many hundreds and probably thousands of British officers and men were alive at that moment who, if it were not for our snipers, would have been killed by the Germans. Mrs Ward quite saw the force of this argument and wrote a most admirable account of her visit to the school. I saw this in proof, but when it appeared the censors had clearly cut out a certain amount. Why they had cut it out no one could ever tell. We had at that time a good number of snipers' robes of painted canvas at the school. The Germans had somewhat similar robes and both sides knew that the other was using them; but the British Censorship would never allow any mention of these robes. You might mention something really important, some new invention, or the effect of some new bullet, or any other matter, which would be of real assistance to the Germans, but these robes were the one thing, which seemed to interest the Press Censorship. Speaking as an Officer-in-charge of a very technical branch of work, I can only say that the Censorship was at times just like an ostrich hiding its head in the sand.

Mrs Humphry Ward went over the whole school, and I must say that her questions probed our work more deeply than those of the average sightseeing officer who visited us.

Apart from visitors who came for various purposes to see the school, we had also several officers who came on duty. Among these was Colonel the Hon T F Fremantle, now Lord Cottesloe. Lord Cottesloe knew more of telescopic sights and rifle shooting than did any of us at the school, and there can be no doubt whatever that his visit was of the greatest assistance to us, With him came Lieutenant-Colonel Robinson, who was in charge of the manufacture of telescopic sights at Enfield and who did so much to assist us in a hundred different ways. I never had the opportunity of visiting the school in England of which Lord Cottesloe was the Commandant, but I had many officers and men who had received a sound grounding there.

Lieutenant-Colonel P W Richardson, the well-known Bisley shot, also visited the school. He was interested in sniping from the very earliest days and was probably the first officer to advocate schools for the teaching of shooting with telescopic sights.

One evening after the school had been running well over a year, I was sitting by the mess-room fire when a couple of officers were shown in. Both were wearing Burberrys, so that I was not able to see their rank, but both were very young looking. One of them said: "We looked in to have a talk to you about schools, for we are going to start one. What we want to know is, how this school manages to get everyone who comes to it so damned keen on their job?"

I pointed out that we had a really interesting subject to teach and enlarged upon the great theory that I always used to hold that you did not want to have officers on a course too near a big town. If you have a good subject to teach, and can teach it intelligently, you ought to be able to interest them enough in the course to keep their minds at work, especially if you have at least two hours' games for those who want

Find the sniper (the flat cap gives him away)

them every afternoon. If you are near a big town, it means dinners and sweet champagne, and other things, which do not conduce to accurate shooting. Our school was rather more than four kilometres from Aire, and no one was allowed to go there without a pass. A pass could be had by any officer for the asking, but I found that, once the course got its grip, except on Sunday, Aire was very little visited.

My two visitors then ran through the curriculum of the school with me, and as the room was hot, removed their Burberrys. I then realized how great a compliment had been paid to the School, for both were regular soldiers of long service – as I could tell from their decorations and medals – and high rank. Presently, they went, and I never saw them again, nor did I learn their names, but we always thought that their visit was about the highest compliment ever paid to the First Army School of SOS.

One point that certainly struck us in our first coming to Linghem was the delight of the inhabitants in getting a permanent school quartered in their village. This, of course, meant prosperity to them. They had previously had one or two battalions, and there was still a large notice affixed on one of the houses, "Billet Officer," but when we came they had had no British soldiers for the last six months. We were welcomed with open arms. White wine, which started the war at 90 centimes, was 1.50 a bottle. Eggs, fruit, and everything else were cheap. When we left in 1918, that same white wine was 10 francs a bottle, and even a potato was hard indeed to come by.

We owed much to the courtesy of the Secretary to the Maire, M Huart, who smoothed away every kind of difficulty. That occasional difficulties should arise is natural enough, but the French were for the most part extraordinarily kind. Here and there, of course, one came across difficult people, as for instance, the determined lady who, when a Portuguese class was quartered in the village, finding that they drank no beer at her *estaminet* – for the Portuguese do not drink beer, and the 10 franc vin blanc was rather beyond them – refused to allow them to draw water at her well, although it was the only decent one in the village. I had an interview with the lady, at which she wept copious floods of tears, and said that the Sergeant who had reported the matter to me was a *diable*, who had always disliked her from the first day that he saw her. But she ultimately, of course, had to give in, under threat of having a permanent guard placed upon the well.

I have often marvelled how little friction there really was between the French and us. If a French Army were quartered in England in the same way that we were quartered in France, I do not for a moment believe that our people would show towards them the same kindness and consideration which we received from the French.

When Gray and I had spent seven very strenuous weeks at the Army School, we were both granted eight days' leave. Immediately on our return, we were inspected by Sir Henry Horne, the new Army Commander, who came out many times afterwards. It was always a matter of pride to the School to have some new thing to show to the Army Commander. On one occasion Lord Horne inspected some Lovat Scouts whom we were training as reinforcements for our Army Groups, and after this an order came through to us to hold ourselves ready to train all reinforcements for Lovat Scouts throughout the BEF. How much Lord Horne did to encourage and help the School no words can describe.

At this time also, or a little later, Major-General Hastings Anderson was appointed Chief of Staff at First Army Headquarters.

Chapter Five

Some Sniping Memories

When first I came into the First Army area, the main point, which struck me, was the difference between the trenches where my work now lay and those of the Third Army. The Third Army had, of course, taken over from the French, and their trenches were really in the nature of deep ditches, without any vast amount of sandbags. Sometimes these trenches extended through a clayey formation, but more often they were in chalk. This chalk made front line observation in the bright sunlight somewhat trying, as there was always a dazzle in the rays reflected from the white background. In the Third Army area also the ground was rolling, and it was nearly always possible to obtain some kind of a position of vantage behind the parados. For this purpose I had had a special portable loophole made, shaped something in the form of a wide triangle, but the back shutter of which slid along in grooves. This back shutter was made of steel and formed a very fine protection, as even if an enemy sniper put a bullet through the front loophole, the bullet was stopped by the sliding shutter behind, unless, that is, the shot happened to be fired – a twenty to one chance – along the exact line in which one was looking through the two loopholes. A good many of these loopholes were used in the Third Army, but I found that conditions in the First Army rendered them of no great value.

The First Army were holding from just south of Armentieres down to Vimy Ridge, and subsequently it held almost to Arras, but at this time their lines did not stretch so far south. All the northern part of their trench system was in an absolutely flat plain, where trenches were shallow owing to the presence of water at no great depth underground, and were really much more in the nature of breastworks. In most places, it was useless to go out behind the parados, as the ground was so low that you got no view. This refers, at any rate, to all the northern line, after which we entered the coal region, where posts could be dug in the slagheaps and in the ruins of shelled buildings. As a rule, to put a post in a shelled building in the northern part of the line was simply to court disaster, as these buildings, where they were near enough to the line to admit of sniping, were continually shelled and sprayed with machine-gun bullets. But further south, buildings were more common and might be made use of. As a rule, however, I found that the placing of sniping posts in either buildings or trees was a mistake. For once such posts were discovered by the enemy, he had little difficulty in ticking them off on his map and demolishing them. Of course the same was true of posts in more open ground, but these were much harder to spot, and it is better to be shelled in the open ground than in a house where you are liable to be hurt by falling bricks, etc.

The problem then that the First Army line presented was an interesting one, and I have always thought it much the most difficult line to organize for sniping of which I had knowledge.

Having learned my work in the trenches of the Third Army, I found that in the First Army I had first of all to unlearn a great deal. The problem was essentially different, but after a year's experience, during which practically every portion of the Front was visited, one collected a great number of ruses and plans. Still, at first, to put a concealed loophole into the Fauquissart or Neuve Chapelle breastworks was a really difficult problem, which indeed was only solved when, as I have explained in an earlier chapter, "Gray's Boards" were invented. These were immediately successful, and from the time that they were first used, it was easier to make a good loophole in the breastworks than in any other part of our line.

There were, here and there, all along the Army front, what may be known as "bad spots," that is, places where, through some advantage of ground, the enemy dominated us. In such places our snipers had to redouble their efforts, and even then the enemy remained a thorn in our sides. There were other places, of course, where we had an equivalent advantage, and there we were soon able to force the Germans to live an absolutely troglodytic existence. In fact orders were published in the German army on some fronts that when a man was off duty he was to remain in a dugout.

Of course the greatest difficulty that we had was the continual movement of divisions. A division would just be settling down comfortably and getting its sniping into good order, when it would be ordered to depart to another Army, and the incoming division would almost always succeed in giving away some of the posts. This was a necessary evil, and could not be helped, but the advent of a single really bad sniping division gave an immense amount of extra work. It was exactly as if a party of really capable sportsmen were shooting an area for big game, or, better still, a Scottish deer forest. Imagine these sportsmen replaced by careless and ignorant tourists. The ground would inevitably be maltreated, the wrong beasts shot, corries shot when the wind was unfavourable, and all the deer stampeded onto the next forest. Of course, in this case, the deer did not stampede, but plucked up courage and shot back.

This condition of things was, of course, impossible to remedy, but we were luckier than other Armies, since our southern wing was formed by the Canadian Corps, who had the same trenches for fifteen months, and who never changed their divisions. In this corps many of the reliefs worked beautifully, the incoming and the outgoing sniping officers being thoroughly in accord with each other. Major Armstrong, a well-known British Columbian big game shot, was Corps Sniping Officer, and there was no keener.

Of course it must be understood, as I have tried to explain before, that in writing this book, I realize that my point of view is an exceedingly narrow one and that I look at everything from the point of an officer whose business it was to consider sniping, observation and scouting of paramount importance. We were continually getting new snipers who took the places of those who had either become casualties or had been put to other work. New snipers were nearly always optimistic, and it was quite a common thing for them to think that they were doing the enemy much more damage than was really the case. A conversation has been known to run as follows:

"Morning, you two."

"Good morning, sir."

"Anything doing?"

"Smith got a 'un this morning, sir."

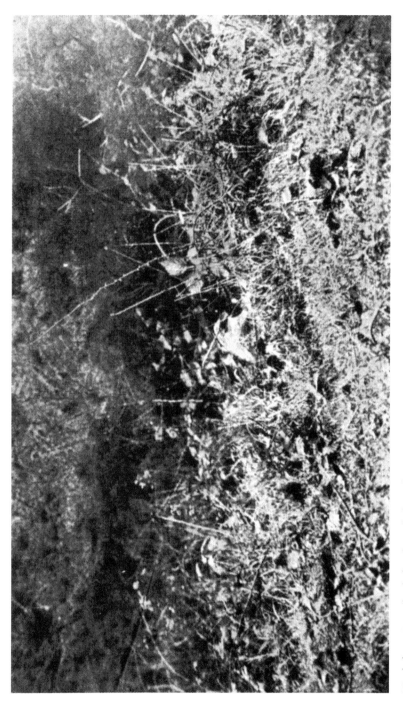

Find the sniper (look for the rifle barrel)

"Good. How do you know?"

"He give a cry, threw up his hands and fell back."

Now this may have been correct, but, as a matter of fact, continued observation showed that a man shot in ordinary trench warfare very very rarely either threw up his hands or fell back. He nearly always fell forward and slipped down. For this the old Greek rendering is best, "And his knees were loosened."

We soon found that a very skilled man with a telescope could tell pretty accurately whether a man fired at had been hit, or had merely ducked, and this was the case even when only the "head of the target" was visible; but to be certain of his accuracy, it was necessary that the observer should have had a long experience of his work, coupled with real aptitude for it. The idea of how to spot whether a German was hit or not was suggested by big-game shooting experiences. An animal, which is fired at and missed, always stands tense for the fraction of a second before it bounds away, but when an animal is struck by the bullet there is no pause. It bounds away at once on the impact, or falls. Thus, a stag shot through the heart commences his death rush at once, to fall dead within fifty yards, whereas a stag missed gives that telltale sudden start.

In dealing with trench warfare sniping, a very capable observer soon learned to distinguish a hit from a miss, but there were naturally many observers who never reached the necessary degree of skill. A reason once advanced for claiming a hit was that the Germans had been shouting for stretcher-bearers, but a question as to what was the German word for stretcher-bearer brought confusion upon the young sniper, whose talents were promptly used elsewhere!

But taken long by broad, the accuracy of the information given by snipers was really wonderful. On one occasion the snipers of the 33rd Division reported that two Germans had been seen with the number 79 upon their helmets. This information went from Battalion, through Brigade, Division and Corps, to Army, who rather pooh-poohed the snipers' accuracy, as the 79th, when last heard of, had been upon the Russian front. Within a day or two, however, the Germans opposite the battalion to which these snipers belonged sent a patrol out of their trenches one misty morning. The patrol fell in with our scouts, who killed two and carried back the regulation identifications. These proved the sentries to be correct.

It was in the same Division that in one tour of duty the snipers reported the cap-bands of the Germans opposite as: (1) brown; (2) yellow; (3) white. This again raised a doubt as to their accuracy; the matter was interesting, as it seemed possible that the trenches had been taken over by dismounted Uhlans. But before long the snipers were once again justified. A prisoner was taken, who acknowledged that the men of his unit had, under orders, covered the state badges on their caps with strips of tape wound round and round the brims. Prior to putting on this tape, he said, many of his comrades had dipped it in their coffee.

It is only fair to say that the sniping officer of the division in question was Lieutenant Gray, and the exceeding skill of the officers and men under him may fairly be laid at his door.

There was in the trenches a very simple way of testing the accuracy of the sniper's observation. The various German States, Duchies or Kingdoms all wore two badges on their caps, one above the other, the higher being the Imperial badge and the lower the badge of the State. Thus, the Prussian badge is black and white,

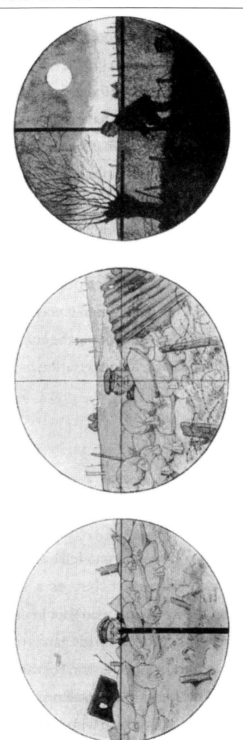

Telescopic sights. Diagrams showing point of aim.
From left to right: 1. With Periscopic Prism – Aldis. 2. With Winchester. 3. With German telescopic sight (showing use at night).

the Bavarian light blue and white; the Saxon, green and white. These badges or, to be more correct, cockades, are not larger than a shilling, and the colours are in concentric rings. A series of experiments carried out at First Army School by the Staff and some of the best Lovat Scouts proved that these colours were indistinguishable with the best Ross telescope at a distance of more than 150 yards, except under the most favourable circumstances. So if ever a sniper (who, of course, knew what troops he was faced by) reported the colours of cockades when more than 150 yards from the enemy, it was at once clear that his imagination was too strong to admit of his useful employment with an observer's telescope.

Another great duty of snipers was the blinding of the enemy. Thus, if the Germans bombarded any portion of our front, their artillery observers almost always did their work from the flank, where very often from the front line or from some other point of vantage they spotted and corrected the shell bursts of their gunners. On such occasions, our snipers opposite both flanks of the bombarded area broke the periscopes of the German observers and thus often succeeded in either rendering them blind, or forcing them to take risks.

When Germans retaliated and shot our periscopes, we had a number of dummies made, and by taking the entry and exit of the bullet through the back and front of these, we were able to spot many posts from which the Germans were firing. The result was that the enemy suffered casualties. It is, in fact, not too much to say that in these ways we were able from very early days to place the position of any sniper who troubled us, and, once placed, there were many methods by which the man could be rendered harmless.

Another point that was not without interest was the fact that occasionally, and apparently for no reason, the Germans sighted their rifles by firing at marks upon our parapets. If they did this in a high wind, it might have been possible that they were trying to get the correct wind allowance to put on their rifles; but as they often did it, and it happened all along the line on a still morning, we felt we must seek some other explanation. Collaboration with intelligence proved that this orgy of rifle sighting seemed to coincide with the relief by one battalion of another in the trenches. It was one of the many little straws, which showed which way the wind was blowing.

The psychology of the different races of snipers was always interesting. The English were sound, exceedingly unimaginative, and very apt to take the most foolish and useless risks, showing their heads unnecessarily and out of a kind of unthinking optimism. Nor did the death of their comrades cause them to keep their heads down, except in the particular place where a man had been killed. Unimaginativeness is a great quality in war, but when one is playing a very close game, in which no points can be given away, between skilled antagonists as we were doing in sniping, one sometimes wished for a little less woodenheaded "bravery" so-called and a little more finesse.

The Welsh were very good indeed, their 38th Division keeping a special sniper's book, and their sniping officer, Captain Johnson, was very able. I think that in early 1918, the snipers of this Division had accounted for 387 Germans in trench-warfare.

The Canadians, the Anzacs, and the Scottish Regiments were all splendid, many units showing an aggressiveness, which had the greatest effect on the *morale* of the enemy. Of the Australians I had, to my deep regret, no experience, but they always had the name of being very good indeed.

The Americans were also fine shots, and thoroughly enjoyed their work, but my experience of them lay simply in teaching at the school, and I never had the opportunity of seeing them in action.

Of the Germans as a whole one would say that, with certain brilliant exceptions, they were quite sound, but rather unenterprising, and that as far as the various tribes were concerned, the Bavarians were better than the Prussians, while some Saxon units were really first-rate.

I remember once being in the trenches at Ploegsteert Wood, where the Saxons were against us, and our fellows were talking about them being "good old fellows." All the same, it did not do to show the breadth of your forehead to the "good old fellows," for they were really admirable shots. Somehow or other this idea of the "good old fellow" rather stuck in my mind, and I used to picture Fritz the sniper as a stout and careful middle-aged man, who sat in his steel box with a rifle, took no chances, and carried on his work like a respectable tradesman. This idea of the fat bearded sniper, however, was not supported by the telescope, through which I saw some of the most desperate and bedraggled-looking snipers that one could wish to see. Those who sometimes got outside their own lines were, however, I think, rather the "wild boys." After we got rid of them, the Germans fell back upon a kind of sober rifle fire, which made up the main bulk of their sniping.

One point that was noticeable was the good focusing powers of the German snipers of certain regiments, who shot very well before dawn and towards dark. In the very crack Jäger regiments, such regiments as were, I suppose, recruited from Rominten or Hubertusstock districts, where the great preserves of the Kaiser lay and in which were a large percentage of Forest Guards, this was very noticeable. But for long distance work, and the higher art of observation, the Germans had nothing to touch our Lovat Scouts. This is natural enough when one comes to consider the dark forests in which the German Forest Guards live, and in which they keep on the alert for the slightest movement of deer or boar. Mostly game is seen within fifty or seventy yards, or even closer, in these sombre shades, and then it is only the twitching of an ear or the movement of an antler lifted in the gloaming. Compare the open Scottish hills. It was the telescope against the field glass, and the telescope won every time. In fact, in all the time I was in the trenches, I never saw a German telescope, whereas I saw hundreds and hundreds of pairs of field glasses.

Now the best field glass cannot compare with the telescope. Anyone who has tried to count the points on the antlers of a stag will know this. I had a great deal of difficulty in convincing some of our officers, who were used to field-glasses, of this fact, but there was near by the place at which I was quartered in early days the carved figure of a knight in armour standing on the top of a chateau. This knight had very large spurs, and I would ask student officers to try and count the rowels with their field glasses. They never could do so. I would then hand them one of my beautiful Ross glasses, and there always came the invariable question, "Where can I get a glass like this?"

The telescope sight, of course, made accurate shooting in the half-lights very much easier, and indeed for some valuable minutes after it had become too dark to use open sights the telescope sights still gave a clear definition. At night they were invaluable. With a large telescope sight which magnified five times, and which was very kindly lent me by Lady Graham of Arran, several of us succeeded in making a six-inch group on the target at a hundred yards by moonlight, and even by starlight once we made a two and a half-inch group. I tried hard to get an issue of somewhat similar sights for night firing authorized, for when you think of the large amount of coming and going which continues all night behind an occupied trench, there is no doubt that plenty of targets are always presenting themselves. Even the Government issue of telescopic sights were quite useful at night, but their effect would have been many times increased had it been possible to fit them for this purpose with a large object glass.

On both sides, thousands upon thousands of lives were saved by wind, since it was not easy to judge its strength in the trenches. As the targets aimed at were usually only half a head, the very smallest error of judgment resulted in a miss. Once a bullet had whizzed by a German's ear within a few inches, a second exposure of the head was rarely made in the same place.

Trench sniping was, in fact, as defined by Colonel Langford Lloyd, "the art of hitting a very small object straight off and without the advantage of a sighting shot."

At a certain spot in our lines not very far from Auchonvillers, known to fame as "Ocean Villas," a German sniper had done fell work. It is hard to say how many British lives he had taken, but his tally was not small. He lurked somewhere in the mass of heaps of earth, rusty wire and sandbags which there formed a strong point of the German line. There were twenty or thirty loopholes from which he might be firing. The problem was from which of these did his shots actually come? The Germans had a trick of multiplying their loopholes in this fashion. Many steel plates were shoved up on the parapet in the most obvious positions. These were rarely shot through, but they were certainly sometimes used. The German argument must have been that if you have thirty loopholes, it is thirty-to-one against the particular one from which you fire being under observation at that particular moment.

On our side there was no loophole whatever covering the area in which this German sniper worked, and any attempt to spot his post had perforce to be done over the top of the parapet. As he was simply waiting and watching for people to look over, it was only a very hurried and cursory glance that could be taken. At length, however, the Hun was located by an officer, in the vicinity of two enormous steel plates set near the top of his parapet.

As I have said, there was no loophole upon our side, so orders were given that one should be put in during the night right opposite to those two big plates. The next morning it was hardly light when the German sniper shot into our new loophole, which was at once closed. The trap was now ready, and the officer whose duty it was to deal with the matter went one hundred yards down the trench to the right flank, while an assistant protruded the end of a black stick which he happened to have in his hand, keeping at the same time well to the side. At the same moment the officer on the flank shot at the right hand of the two big plates once, and then again. The bullets rang aloud upon the plates, and the German sniper at the second shot betrayed himself. Thinking as he did that the shots were fired from the open loophole opposite to him, he fired at it, and the gas from his rifle gave away his position. The two big plates were, of course, dummies, and he was firing almost from ground level, and from an emplacement cleverly concealed by a mass of broken wire. The loophole was now shut for a moment or two, and then once again opened, the officer on the flank having moved to a position where he could command the German sniper's loophole. His cap had fallen off. He had a bald head. Once found, and unaware of the fact, the sniper was soon dealt with.

One could relate very many such incidents, but they are rather grisly. Sooner or later nearly every troublesome German sniper met his fate.

But the duty of the sniper changed as the war went on. At first his job was to dominate the German snipers, destroy their morale, and make life secure for his own comrades. At the same time there was his Intelligence work. Later, as the warfare became more open, he proved his value over and over again in attack. When a trench was taken, it was his duty to get out in front and (lying in a shell-hole) to keep the enemy heads down while his companions consolidated the newly-won position. When an advance was held up by a machine-gun, it was the sniper's business to put it out of action if he could, and the list of VC's and DCM's, as well as thousands of deeds of nameless men, prove how often he was successful. In the last advance of the Canadian Corps, their very skilled sniping officer, Major Armstrong, told me that a single sniper put out of action a battery of 5.9 guns, shooting down one after another the German officer and men who served it – a great piece of work, and one thoroughly worthy of General Currie's splendid Corps.

But the machine-gun was the sniper's special target. Once, of course, a machine-gun was spotted, or moved in the open, a single sniper was quite capable of putting it out of action. In fact, the sniper's duties were legion. He had to be a really high-class shot, a good and accurate observer, and a good judge of distance, wind and light. Suffice it that in the more open warfare many a sniper killed his fifty Germans in a single day, and whether as a rifleman or scout, he bore a part more perilous than that of the rank and file of his comrades. If you who read this know a man who served his year or two in the sniping section of his battalion, you know one whom it is well that you should honour.

A position, which was much used by German snipers, is supposed to have been trees. This was the theme of many pictures in the illustrated papers, but as a matter of fact a high tree makes a wretched sniping post, and I rarely allowed one to be used on our side. The Germans, however, did extensively use the pollard willows, which were so common a feature on the First Army front. We did not use them, as I have said, but we found that the German sense of humour appears to be much tickled by seeing, or thinking he sees, a Britisher falling out of a tree. When our sniping became very good, and the enemy consequently shy of giving a target, a dummy in a tree worked by a rope sometimes caused Fritz and Hans to show themselves unwisely.

When the sniping was of high class on both sides, all kinds of ruses were employed to get the other side to give a target. But one had to be very careful not to go too far in this sort of work or trickery, lest a *minenwerfer* should take his part in the duel.

From time to time wild geese crossed the trenches in the winter, and their appearance was usually a signal for a fusillade in which every rifle and machine-gun that could be brought to bear on both sides took part. Very rarely was one brought down, though it is possible that along the whole front in the years of war a dozen may have been killed. One in particular, on a wild and stormy evening, was shot by the British and fell in the German lines. The enemy the next day hoisted a sign on which was painted in English the words: "So many thanks!" – which was indeed hard to bear!

There is another incident into which birds also came, which occurred on the Brick-stacks front of the First Army. It was when our sniping had reached its high-water mark in the 11th Corps. Not very long before we had been dominated on this front, but the 33rd Division had put all that right.

One day Lieutenant Gray was coming down the trenches on a tour of inspection, when he found a private soldier with five partridges lying before him on the fire step.

"How did you get them?" said Gray.

"Shot them, sir."

"Yes, but I mean how did you get their bodies?"

"Crawled out, sir, and picked them up."

"By daylight, and in full view of the Germans?"

"Yes, sir. It's all right, sir; they never shoot now."

Gray gave the private in question a good dressing down, but the incident was not without its significance.

One day in 1915, I was knocking about on the top of Hill 63 with a telescope. The edge of Ploegsteert Wood abuts upon this hill, and as I came up I saw an old cock pheasant walking about. At that moment a shell burst very close to him. He was not hit, but he was certainly, very much dazed, for he stood stupidly watching the fumes rising from the cavity. Had it not been for the strict orders concerning game – and the probable arrival of more shells – I could easily have captured him; but after a few moments, during which he sat with his feathers all fluffed out, he gathered himself together and disappeared into the nearest thicket.

I was always very much afraid all through the war that, having started poison gas, the Germans might start using shotguns loaded with buckshot for work between the trenches. Had they done so, patrolling would have become a horrible business; but I suppose that they were restrained by the fact either that such weapons are not allowed by the Geneva Convention, or that the British Isles have such a supply of shotguns and cartridges that the advantage would not remain long upon their side. As it was, things were much more satisfactory, for there was plenty of excitement out in No Man's Land, what with machine-gun bullets and rifle fire, without the added horror of a charge of small shot in the face.

I have touched on the work of observers in the front line in this chapter, but it will be more fully considered in the next upon the subject of Observation, to which this side of the sniper's work really belongs.

Chapter Six

An Observer's Memories

As I have already said, when sniping was started in the BEF, we owed our fairly rapid and certainly very definite success in the task of dominating the Hun to a single factor. Whereas the German sniper usually worked alone, we put up against him two men, one of whom, "A," used the telescope and kept a close watch for "targets" upon a good sector of the enemy's line, while "B," his comrade, used the rifle and shot at the "targets" which "A" found. The result was that at a hundred points along the line you could daily hear a conversation such as this:

A – "Black Sandbags – left – two feet – 'alf a 'Un's 'ead showing. D! he's down!"

B – "Hope he'll come up again."

A – "He's up!"

B (Fires).

A – "Close shave – six inches high – bad luck, ole son!"

Now the total result of the above passage was in all probability not only that a German in the trench opposite had been fired at and missed, but that "A," the telescope man, had seen certain details, which might prove of interest. These details "A," at once, as a matter of routine, entered in his logbook. He enters the time – 11.18 am let us say. The place is C3d.25.85 on the squared map. So far all was simple; but the next entry as to what he had seen was important. A Hun's head, or a yellow-bearded Hun, or an ugly Hun, meant nothing; but a Hun wearing a Prussian cockade, or a Hun wearing a helmet with No 119 on the cover – these things were of importance, and soon, under instruction, sniper-observers gave up reporting black-bearded Germans who leaned over the parapet, and realized the value of the all-important game of identification. They entered besides the details already given, a note of the action taken and the result: in the case we have imagined, "Fired one shot – missed."

It will be further understood that a sniper's observer (and do not forget that the observer's work is much the more trying, and that "A" and "B" change places every twenty minutes to rest the observer's eyes), saw a great many things happen in the enemy lines which did not come under the heading of "targets." Earth being thrown up usually meant work in progress. The occurrence was, of course, noted down in the logbook, with a map reference at which it took place and the spot, if worthwhile, bombarded with trench mortars. Or the observer might spot a machine-gun emplacement, or locate a *minenwerfer*.

But it will be seen that the possibilities are endless, and, as the war went on, the snipers provided a mass of detail, much of which was confirmed by raids and identifications taken from prisoners or from the dead, and very little could happen near the enemy's front lines without our Intelligence being at once aware of it.

An interesting question, which arose, was whether a sniper should enter deductions as well as facts in his reports, and this question was often asked me. The reply was that he should invariably do this provided he marked his deductions very clearly as such.

The most brilliant piece of deduction that I came across was that of an officer in the Royal Warwickshire Regiment, and it had a remarkable sequel. At one point of a supposed disused trench, a cat was observed sunning itself upon the parados. This was duly reported by the observant sniper, and in his logbook for three or four days running came a note of this tortoise-shell cat sunning itself, always at the same spot.

The Intelligence and Sniping Officer of the battalion, on reading his entries, made his deduction, to wit, that the cat probably lived near by. Now at that part of the British line there was a terrible plague of rats, which was probably at least as troublesome upon the German side. So our officer deduced that the cat was a luxury, and that this being so, it had most certainly been commandeered or annexed by enemy officers and probably lived in some enemy officer's headquarters – possibly a company commander's dugout.

Some aeroplane photographs were next taken and studied, with a result that an enemy headquarters was discovered, located and duly dealt with by one of the batteries of howitzers, which made a specialty of such shoots.

I give the full details of this incident in a later chapter. In fact, in trench warfare there was a great deal of scope for deduction.

At one time, before the Germans received the large numbers of light machine-guns which were issued in the later stages of the war, their heavier weapons were mounted in fixed posts, which were very carefully concealed. Sometimes these guns fired a burst at night, and we invented a way in which it was possible to locate them. We had a large tin structure, shaped like an oblong box and made of three walls of tin, each some inches apart. This was mounted on straight square sticks fixed at either end of the box. These sticks fitted into grooves, which were nailed on boards set into the parapet, and after dark were run up until the tin box was above the parapet. Should it in this position happen to catch even one bullet of a burst of fire, as an enemy machine-gun sprayed our trench, it was only necessary to slide down the legs through the grooves, and to place a periscope in front of any hole the machine-gun bullets had made. In this way, the observer found himself looking down the course along which the bullet had come, directly at the spot from which it was fired.

This was rather a clumsy and very uncertain device, but it was used in a dozen other forms. Had it been invented earlier, before the issue of light machine-guns which I have referred to above, it might have been quite valuable, but it came too late, and was soon discarded.

To spot a hostile machine-gun emplacement was one of the most valuable services a front-line observer could render, since of course a single machine-gun can hold up an attack and inflict great casualties. Therefore, when a machine-gun emplacement was spotted it was not necessarily put out of action at once, but its map reference was noted and sent to Intelligence, where it was filed, and action taken by the divisional artillery at the correct time, usually just before a raid or an attack.

On the 11th Corps front in 1916, our troops were continually making raids, and there was a great deal of competition as to who should make the most successful. The result was that the enemy was kept continually upon the jump. The Germans were allowed very little sleep during those months.

One night they decided to try and regain the lost initiative, and a German raid was turned on, which, however, did not meet with great success; in fact, things began to be critical for the raiders, and the German Company Commander in charge came out into No Man's Land to see for himself what was amiss. There in No Man's Land he was killed by our men, and from his body a map was taken on which the position of no less than eighty machine-gun emplacements was marked. At first it was thought that the map on which these eighty emplacements were described might be a fake intended to mislead us, but on comparing it with the emplacements discovered during the previous weeks it was found that no fewer than forty-two of the eighty had been spotted and ticked off, though as yet no serious action against them had been taken.

Such a chance never comes twice, and a few nights later the gunners blew up all the machine-gun emplacements while the South Wales Borderers went across and raided the German trenches. To such a tune was the raid carried out that, though a record number of prisoners were brought in, the raiding party suffered hardly any loss themselves.

More than one officer in the war must have found himself in a dreadful position when captured by the enemy with important maps of his own lines in his pocket. Carelessness, darkness, or misadventure might each or any of them be responsible, but bad as was the lot of the ordinary prisoner, how much worse was that of one whose capture had given valuable local information to the enemy! It is too painful a subject to pursue.

Many people seem to think that all observation is now done from aeroplanes, but this is absurd. The airmen can spot hostile concentrations and do invaluable work in a hundred ways, but, as the war went on, more and more was it recognized how necessary was the ground-observer, for he looked at the enemy from a different angle, and his reports were often of the highest value.

Once the Germans started a new and large form of periscope, and we ceased destroying them at once the moment a clever observer found that with the telescope he could read the reflection of the numbers on the shoulder straps of the Germans who used them, thereby allowing us to identify the opposing unit with both comfort and ease.

It was perhaps natural enough that when a sniper first won his way, into the sniping section of his battalion, he should desire to shoot rather than to observe, yet, as a matter of fact, the observer's was, in my opinion, the post of honour. It was very hard work too, especially in summer time, and more especially still in the chalk country. Some of the happiest days of our lives were spent with the Ross telescope, either watching the German lines from the front trenches or from some observation post further back overlooking the wide areas that lay behind them. On many occasions one became so interested that meals were forgotten, as the telescope searched and waited for the artillery observers' observation posts.

Such a one there was at Beaumont Hamel. It was in the autumn of 1915, and the leaves were falling, which is the best time of all for spotting the posts of enemy observers. Right back in the village was a building, which, though it had been heavily shelled, still stood in a fairly commanding position. A direct hit had at some previous time smashed a jagged hole under the eaves through which one could see a beam stretching across. It was the presence of this beam, which first drew attention to the spot, for it seemed strange that the shell should not have carried it away. It looked, indeed, as if it had been placed there afterwards; but it was a little back in the room behind, and it was difficult to tell whether the shell might not have left it intact.

In the morning, when the light was bad owing to the position of the sun, it was very hard to spot the shell hole, and the beam was invisible, but one day when the light was very good in the afternoon, the glass revealed five bricks standing on this broken beam. Natural enough – but not quite so natural when the next day the five bricks had changed their position. On the first day, four had been lying along the beam at full length and one was set upon its end. On the second day, a second had adopted the erect position. Late in the afternoon of that clear day, the officer who had observed and who was taking interest in the five bricks saw through his 30-power glass a German hand moving the bricks and the light glint on a pair of German field-glasses levelled amongst them.

The second shell from our gunners removed forever that post of Beaumont Hamel.

That was one side of the game.

The other as when your own post got given away – as it sometimes did – usually by the flash of a glass in some unskilled hands, by aeroplane photographs, or by some idiot approaching the post when the light allowed of good observation from the German line. Then the first news you had of it was the arrival of the German shells. Followed either the decision to stick it, or the climb, during the later stages of the war in a gas mask, down the ladder and a dash for the nearest dugout.

Once on a certain famous ridge riddled with our observation posts, I can remember finding a path leading to every post clear in the new fallen snow, and a German aeroplane imminent overhead. Now supposing that plane happened to be a photographic plane, as it most probably was, the whole of the posts would be given away as clearly as if we had sent a map across with them marked upon it.

I can remember how we made false trails in little parties, and never did soldiers double at a faster pace! A fall of snow helped us a great deal as far as aeroplane photographs were concerned, and no doubt the Germans also, but even at such times the German flying man did not come much over our lines.

There was another post, which we used for a long time, the only road to which lay along a disused trench in which were several deep shell holes. As this trench was full of a kind of thick dust or mud according to the weather, and as the whole length of it had to be passed over by crawling there was great fear that the trails of the observers would one day be photographed from the air. At one point, therefore, an entrenching tool was left with which each observer obliterated his trail as far as he could. One becomes very careful in these small details when one's life hangs upon the issue.

Perhaps the most remarkable observation posts used during the war were three famous ones in the French lines. At one point there was a slight rise in front of the French position and above the German. Both trenches cut across the Paris road, and exactly upon the top of the rise between the trenches where the observation was best stood a milestone on which was stated the number of kilometres to Paris.

This milestone the French photographed. The photograph was sent to the Camouflage Works, where an exact copy of the milestone, with the number of kilometres printed on it, was made in steel, but with an observation eye-slit covered with gauze. Then one night a French party crept out and removed the real milestone, putting in its stead the camouflaged one. A tunnel from the trench was next dug, and for many months inside that harmless-looking milestone a pair of keen French eyes noted much of interest that happened in the German line.

In another case, a huge dead, yellow-bearded Prussian lay, on a point of vantage, staring at the sky. He, too, was photographed and copied, and from the hollow shell, clothed in his uniform, another observer fulfilled his duty. A dead horse likewise was replaced and used.

In fact, the romance of observation was endless, forming, as it did, one of the more human phases of the world war. For here, at least, an observer's life was often dependent upon his own skill. Observers often lay in full view, their lives depending upon quiescence and their art of blending with the background.

When, at a later date, there was an issue in the British Army of sniping robes for the use of snipers and observers-robes which tallied with any background and were ornamented with all kinds of dazzle painting-there was a tendency to send snipers and observers out in front. As a rule I think this was a mistake, for the hours out in front from dawn to dark were very long, and the observer had to keep upon the *qui vive* for too long a period. Also the smallest movement would give him away, and he was rarely in a position to use his telescope over any large area. Freedom of movement is necessary to the observer, and as to the sniper, I always felt that it was wrong to send him out except on a definite quest, for the man behind the trench is always in a superior position to the man who is lying on open ground without any chance of escape.

So far I have dealt with what is known as front line observation; but besides this we have to consider the very wide subject of back area observation. The sniper's duty is to watch the enemy's front and support lines. The brigade observers, if any – and keen brigades were always sending them to be trained – and the divisional observers working from posts on their own support lines, or from some point of vantage far behind, watched the areas lying at the back of the enemy fighting lines as far as the glass could see.

To some of the Army Corps were attached the Lovat Scouts Sharpshooters. This name turned out in a way really a misnomer, for the Lovats were found to be so invaluable with the telescope that they were in many cases forbidden to use the rifle. Many Corps also had groups of observers formed from their Corps Cavalry. Besides these, we had the FOO's and Artillery observers who, however, do not come within the scope of this chapter as their work is so largely for the guns.

In order to understand fully the tremendous mass of work done by observers, you must realize that behind the lines the Major-General, the Corps Commander, the Army Commander and the Commander-in-Chief himself are all blind. Their brains direct the battle, but it is with the eyes of Sandy McTosh that they see. And nobly through the war did Sandy do his part. It is from him and his officers that the blind General behind learns how the battle goes – that the brigade have gained

Inside the Observation Post (from a drawing by Ernest Blaikley)

Lovat Scouts: Battle observers (from a drawing by Ernest Blaikley)

their first objective – that the _th are held up by wire – that at N26, C4.3 at least six German battalions are massing for a counter-attack. In the Vimy Ridge battle did not Lieutenant Whamond and Sergeant Fraser observe, and did not the guns they warned break up, a mighty counter-attack before ever it was launched?

The duty of the battle observer is to obtain the information as to how each phase of the battle goes, and then to get that information back to where it should be of value.

The battle observer's post or, rather, his series of posts, in an advance, may begin in an observation post, proceed forward to a series of shell holes, and finish in a wrecked German lorry stranded upon some convenient slope. He will use the telephone. His runners – who take back his reports when the telephone wires are cut by shell fire – will escape on one occasion almost unshot at; on the next gas shells will pursue them with positive malignancy. The observer cannot observe in his gas mask, so that gas shells are his particular enemy, and in many of the later attacks the Germans at once drenched all possible observation posts with gas.

But, as I say, the observer is the eye of the High Command. Far away a General and his Chief of Staff are looking at a map. An orderly enters and hands over a flimsy to the Chief of Staff. He reads out the message. The General gives a sigh of relief. He knows now that the danger spot is behind the remnants of the gallant battalions of the 381st Brigade. Sandy McTosh has made "siccar" – he has seen – he has verified – he has got his report back. Those eyes, trained on the hill among the deer, may have had their share, and that no small one, in the making of history.

Battle observing was the blue ribbon of observation. Although the first battalion of Lovat Scouts went to Gallipoli, and later to Salonica, only coming to their true work in France in 1918, yet since 1916 this splendid regiment was represented there by the Lovat Scouts Sharpshooters whom I have referred to above, and of whom nine groups, each about twenty strong, and each under an officer, were attached to a certain Army Corps. Every man of these groups was a picked stalker and glassman, and they were used largely for long-range observation.

It fell to the First Army Sniping School to train their reinforcements. Keener men never lived, nor more dependable. I remember once a Zeppelin was reported as falling in the enemy back areas some six or seven thousand yards behind the German line. This report was made by divisional observers, but it was promptly denied by the Lovat Scouts, who stated very gravely that there was a difference between a Zeppelin and a half-deflated. balloon!

Lovat Scouts Sharpshooters were trained at Beauly in map reading, compass work, etc, and first came out in separate groups. A little later Lieutenant-Colonel Cameron of Lochiel arrived in France to co-ordinate their work. At this time their raison d'être was not always apparent to the units to which they were attached, and some of them were put on to observe for enemy aeroplanes, in which work their skill was rather thrown away. But this was largely put right by Lochiel, whose work was invaluable. Later they were under the command of Lieutenant-Colonel Grant, and towards the end of the war, as I have mentioned above, the First Lovat Scouts were brought home from abroad to take up their true work of observation, just the whole period of the war too late.

At first they were quarantined for a time, as most of them were suffering from malaria, and from then onwards tremendous efforts were made to train the whole regiment in the higher forms of map reading. It is, I believe, a fact that it was only on November 11th, the day of the Armistice that the order finally came through from the War Office, which settled the establishment of the Lovat Scouts with the British Expeditionary Force.

The Lovat Scouts were intensely and rightly proud of their regiment and its work. Once I received orders to train forty foreigners as Lovat Scouts, and called up an old Lovat and told him so and ordered him to make certain arrangements.

"Yes, sir," said he and saluted.

One of my officers was lying behind a hedge observing, and on leaving me the old Lovat walked down this hedge soliloquising. He did not see the officer, who, however, overheard his soliloquy. it ran thus:

"Forty Englishmen to be trained as Lovat Scouts! Abominable! – Preposterous! – and it can't be done!"

The 1st Corps had a splendid system under which the Lovat Scouts attached to it worked. It possessed a grand group under Lieutenant Whamond, MC, whose equal at his work I never saw in France. The system was this: Scouts from the group were available on application to the Corps Intelligence Office. Thus, if a battalion had been ordered to raid the enemy trenches, the Commanding Officer of that battalion could indent for some Lovats to go and make a reconnaissance of the enemy wire for him. Or if a Divisional Commander thought the enemy activities increasing, he could obtain some special pairs of Lovats to watch the part of the line he considered threatened. The group, in fact, were at the service of all units in the Corps, and the result was that when they were applied for, their assistance was fully valued, and they went always to a definite job.

Various scouts from this group used to come up to First Army School of SOS to recoup, for, during the long drawn out operations in front of Lens, the continual use of the glass was very trying.

A story, probably apocryphal, was always told in the 1st Corps concerning a gigantic corporal of the Lovats who stood six feet five inches in height and was certainly one of the strongest men in the Army. He was talking with his companion – for the scouts worked in pairs – when his conversation was overheard by some men of a new formation. As the Lovats were speaking Gaelic, these men at once jumped to the conclusion that they were listening to German, and demanded an instant surrender.

The night was dark, but, as the story goes, it was not the new formation who brought back the Lovats as prisoners, but the Lovats who brought back the new formation.

The final arrangement in the BEF, which never took effect, allotted groups of Lovat Scouts to each Division. At each Army there was to be a Major in charge on the Headquarters staff, and a captain at the Corps; but, as I have said, this system had hardly begun to operate when the war ended.

In training glass men, one wonderfully soon realized how impossible it was to teach any man to use his telescope skilfully who had not been accustomed to it from early youth. Every soldier can, of course, be taught which end to look through, and how to focus, and such details, but these men who began late in life never got the same value from their glasses as did the gillies and the stalkers, and from the point of view of accuracy they were in no way comparable. The truth, that to use a stalking telescope well needs just as much time, practice, and natural gift as first-class shooting, was soon recognized, and would-be observers were sent to the First Army School from all over the BEF. But work on them as we would, they never averaged anything like the Lovat standard.

It sounds a bold statement to make, but the Lovats never let one down. If they reported a thing, the thing was as they reported it. Certainly the men who follow the red deer of Scotland proved themselves once again in this war to possess qualities which, let us hope, will never pass from the British race.

As ammunition grew plentiful, and observation more and more adequate, it naturally became less and less healthy for the German to move about in his back areas in daylight. Thus, one day, two officers happened to be in an observation post which was connected with the guns, when out of a wood some thousands of yards behind the German line emerged three figures. The light was beautiful, and as the figures came nearer and nearer, one of the officers began to take an interest.

As a rule, that observation post did not ring up the guns unless a party of Germans over half a dozen in number was seen, but presently the officer at the telescope spoke.

"I say?"

"Yes."

"Get on to Stiggins" (the code name of the battery). "Tell them three Hun officers with blue cloaks lined with light blue silk, blucher boots and shining swords, will be at the cross-roads at H16, C45.5 in about five minutes. Tell them they are probably Prince Eitel Fritz and Little Willie. I will give the word when to let them have it."

Through the glass could be clearly seen – it was afternoon, and the sun was in a perfect position – the nonchalant way in which those three arrogant looking Hun officers stared about as they approached the crossroads.

Then, in due course, the observing officer said: "Now" – and a moment later the shells passed over the observation post with a sound as of the tearing of silk, and the three "princes," blue cloaks and swords were flying at all angles as they dashed back from the cross-roads, only to run into another shell burst. Two fell – the other made good his escape. It was never learned who they were.

Another incident. One very misty day two officers were in an observation post looking out over the huge devastation of the Loos salient. They were not in an artillery, but in an Intelligence observation post, which, however, was linked up with the guns. Suddenly the mist thinned, revealing far behind the German lines, 7,000 yards away, a number of figures engaged in harvesting.

"Ring up 'Compunction,'" said one officer, "and tell them that sixty Huns are working on the corn at U22, A45.70."

"By God, cancel that," cried the other, whose eyes were still on the telescope. "There are women among them."

They were French women, with a sprinkling of Bavarian or Prussian soldiers. The long distance observer saved lives, even behind the Hun lines, as well as took them.

Sometimes it was the observer's duty to watch a single German for days at a time, not for the sake of watching a particular man, but because the man happened perhaps to be a sentry on the particular piece of line which was under observation. I remember watching a German sentry in this way, or, rather, seeing him from time to time from the Monday to the Thursday. He never gave an opportunity for a shot, though periodically he used to peer quickly over the parapet and as quickly subside; but one got quite used to his routine. His dinner was brought him at his post, where he seemed to remain for very long hours. Once a friend, who was engaged in painting a notice, seemed to come and sit and talk with him. The sentry himself was an exceedingly young German, and I should say an extraordinarily bad sentry. He sometimes used to shoot at us if we gave him provocation, but he was an appallingly bad shot. He was so exceedingly young that I was very glad that I had not a rifle with me, for when at last he did give a chance it was the Company-Sergeant-Major, who cared not if he was young or old, who did what was necessary.

There were certain observation posts in or outside the British lines from which no shot was ever allowed to be fired, lest the post should be betrayed, so valuable were they for observation. From one you could see at close range a German mounted military policeman – he was not always mounted – directing the traffic. You could almost see the expression on the faces of the Huns.

At another point an observation post which was linked up with the guns had a long distance view of a straight road near a ridge running behind the German lines, along which even in daylight Huns were wont to move in small bodies.

One day an officer and a corporal were in this post, when the corporal drew the attention of the officer to a single figure moving along the road. By deduction it was that of a German officer, for every now and again he would meet little parties of troops coming along the road in threes and fours, not enough to shoot.

"Sir," said the corporal, "the officer stops each lot and kind of seems to inspect them. I expect he is a disciplinarian."

The officer smiled.

Some little distance further on he knew a point on the road was registered by our guns. Before the officer came to this, he gave the word along the telephone to fire. As the shells approached, the Hun officer hurled himself to the ground, from which, after the smoke cleared from a very nice shot, he was not seen to rise. But the chances are he crawled away. If not, the German Army was certainly short of an officer of "push and go."

Of course the difference between the really skilled observer and the makeshifts who sometimes had to act in their places came out in a very marked degree at the longer ranges. The latter did not understand the telescope, and were never able to focus it so as to get the best results. In fact, when happenings were quite clear to anyone used to the telescope, these men were all at sea and could not distinguish much.

Anyone who was a real artist with the telescope was, of course, always trying different glasses and different magnifications. Apart from the telescopes which I had purchased with Mr St Loe Strachey's invaluable fund, the Lady Roberts fund sent me out a number of very high-class glasses of all magnifications. After a great deal of experimenting, we came to the conclusion that during all the morning hours, when the sun was facing us, we should do best for all our work with a 10-power magnification, whereas, of course, when the sun went round behind us, higher-powered glasses gave better results. Still, it was very rare indeed that it was worthwhile to pull out the 30-power stop. Glasses even of the same magnification vary to an amazing extent. Some are what may be called sweet, that is, easy and restful for the eyes to look through. Others, of perhaps exactly similar type and by the same maker, are hard and unsatisfactory. Most of the Lovat Scouts brought out their own glasses, nearly all Ross's – indeed, I never knew of any glass to compare with those made by this maker.

There was one duty of back area observers, which was always interesting, and this was watching enemy railway crossings. All these crossings were, of course, registered by our guns, and it was the duty of the observer to keep a good look-out on them, and when a train stopped in the station, and consequently a good deal of traffic was held up on either side of the railway crossing, he would ring up the guns. A few well-placed shells would then wreak havoc upon the enemy.

A system, which was extraordinarily clear and interesting, was adopted by one Corps. This Corps had, let us say, five posts manned by observers. All these posts were linked up with artillery. Back at Corps, stretched on an enormous table, was a large map, on which, of course, the five observation posts were marked. The observers in the posts sent in their daily diary of observation, and when anything in it was of importance, it was entered on this large map. Thus, we will call the posts Tiger, Lion, Leopard, Puma and Jaguar, the names by which they were known. Everything observed from Lion was entered in red ink, everything from Tiger in violet, and from the others also in different coloured inks. It was thus possible at a single glance to tell exactly what had been seen during the past week from each post. Of course sometimes two posts observed the same thing, but only on the extreme limits of their area of observation.

A good observation post was a great asset, and sore, indeed, were the observers if it was given away. There was one such post on a certain front, which lay within six hundred yards of the enemy's front line. This post had been used and had remained undiscovered for four months. One day there was some change in the arrangement of Corps, and a smart young staff captain arrived at the post and stated that he had orders to take it over from the observers.

Luckily, the observer officer, who shall be nameless, was in the post, and he is reported to have addressed that staff captain as follows:

"There are two ways, sir, in which this can be done. The one would be if you were to bring me a written authorization from the head of Intelligence in my Corps, telling me to deliver up the post. That would be the proper and official way. The other would be to throw me out. Which are ye for?"

As the speaker was over six feet high and had to pass most doors sideways, he remained in unmolested possession of that post.

One lingers over observation, because it was so intensely interesting. During the long and weary period of trench warfare, when one saw so few Germans in the ordinary course of events, it was delightful to be able to go and look, with the help of a Ross glass, into their private life. Many and many a time did officers say to me that one of the things they most desired and would most enjoy would be to go for a short tour behind the German lines and see what it all looked like. I quite agreed with them, but by the use of the telescope we were able to visualize a great deal of the German common task and daily round.

One early morning, when I was at First Army Sniping School, it became necessary that a recently joined NCO who had just come out from England, should be

The Fatal Cap

what Archibald Forbes' German general called "a little shooted." Almost as soon as it was light we went down to the line and crawled up through a wood, which overlooked the German lines. This wood would have been an almost ideal place for observation, and, indeed, there were two or three observation posts there, but, as usual, some incoming division had wanted some of the material which went to the making of these posts and had torn it from them, thus giving them most royally away. The result was that the woods were by no means a health resort, as one never knew when the Germans would start shelling them.

That summer morning, however, the sun had risen clear and bright, throwing for a short period of time some kind of illusion over the sad and war-worn landscape – for really after two or three years in France one began to feel a horror of broken masonry and the ugly distortion of war. Very rarely was a scene beautiful, on that part of the front at any rate, but on this morning there was a tang in the air, and it was good to be alive. With our telescopes, as soon as we reached a point of vantage, we were able to see various slight movements in the German lines. It was a curiously peaceful movement – fatigue parties moving about carrying large pots full of cooked rations. In front of us and at no great distance there was a little rounded hummock, which had obviously been strengthened with concrete. Two men came up to this, bearing two large pots slung upon a pole between them, and shortly afterwards four more arrived. All went into a concrete fort, which was too large to be a pillbox. I suggested to an officer who was with me that the place ought to be shelled, but he laughed and said: "They have tried it a couple of times, but the shells have simply bounced off. And now they have the place safely registered on the map, and if we come to advance in that quarter we should put some howitzer on to it which would do the work properly."

Some of these German strong posts certainly did need heavy guns to deal with them. No doubt there is a great satisfaction in having an absolutely safe hole into which to creep when artillery fire begins, but it is doubtful whether it is good policy to make too good arrangements of this kind. Many Germans no doubt saved their fives by going down their deep dug-outs and into their concrete pill-boxes, but many more, as is common knowledge, when our men came over, stayed down too long and were bombed to death.

But to return. Lying on that hillside in the early morning has always remained, for no particular reason, one of my most vivid memories in the war, probably because there was no shelling on either side and one had for once the opportunity of watching the enemy moving peacefully about his tasks.

One point that struck me very strongly was the appearance of the Germans, who were certainly very much less smart than our men. The little round caps, which the privates wore always, reminded me of a cook's cap, and if the French steel helmet was a thing of beauty and the British certainly not, the German was hideous beyond words. The colour of the German uniform was splendid and very difficult to pick up.

When in a back area observation post, one was often watching both Germans and British, and there is no question at all that the British were much easier to see than the Germans. This was not because khaki was a bad colour to blend with backgrounds but because the tops of the British caps were all of so much larger area than the German. The flat-topped caps which so many of the British at one time wore were simply an advertisement of their presence, and even the soft caps, for wearing which officers were arrested when on leave by conscientious APM's, were too wide. Any flat surface worn on top of the head is certain to catch every bit of light, and a flash of light means movement, and draws the observer's telescope as a magnet draws metal.

The ideal army, could I clothe it, would wear a very curious shape of cap, with certainly an uneven outline.

But I do not need to labour this point. You have only to look at the photographs contained in this book to see what a terrible handicap a definite outline is.

There was one incident of observation, which, although it did not happen often, gave one a distinct feeling of importance. Most shelling done by the Germans was on registered cross-roads and suchlike spots, and always when they saw a body of men of any size they would, of course, shell it. But the observer, who usually went into his post rather late – as in the early morning observation, owing to the mist and the position of the sun, was impossible – often received the honour of a special shelling all to himself. This was not the usual chance shelling, as that, as I have said, was always done upon the roads, and very often the observer made his way by footpaths or across the open ground.

I think the Germans often suspected observation posts, and they paid a compliment to observers by shelling all those who moved in their neighbourhood.

Chapter Seven

The Curriculum and Work at First Army School of S.O.S.

The making of a good shot in a course of seventeen days is no easy matter. The First Army School of Sniping was, as I have said, founded for the instruction of officers and NCOs who should, in their turn, instruct, and all who came to it were supposed to be already "good shots." As a matter of fact, the standard was wonderfully high, and we very rarely had a hopeless case. Did such a man put in his appearance, there was only one thing to be done, and that was to send him back to his battalion.

Yet although a great mass of good material came to us, we were nearly always able to improve every student's shooting by 30 or 40 per cent. It is wonderful what can be done in seventeen days if both the class and the instructors are working in unison.

Each class used to begin with an inspection of rifles, followed by a lecture on care and cleaning, at which the value of the polished barrel was taught with no uncertain voice.

There were many difficulties in the way of teaching shooting with telescopic sights, when the issue of these was so limited as it was in France. Many times officers who ought to have known better advocated the shooting away of a mass of ammunition through telescope-sighted rifles at ranges of five or six hundred yards. It was hard to make these officers realize that the sole value of a telescopic rifle lay in its extreme accuracy, and that if the rifle were continually fired through, the barrel would become worn. The best shot in the world, were he using it, would find his group spreading ever more widely upon the target. It was necessary, therefore, that the happy mean should be struck, so every officer and NCO who came to the school was ordered to bring with him two rifles, one of them with open sights. Until a man had proved that he could shoot really well with open sights, he was not allowed to touch a telescopic sighted rifle.

As a matter of fact, anyone who can make good shooting with the ordinary service rifle will find very little difficulty in improving his marksmanship when he is promoted to a telescopic sight.

One of the greatest difficulties that we had – the difficulty which literally haunted the whole of instruction in France, was the fact that the telescopic sights were set, not on top, but at the left-hand side of the rifle. This caused all kinds of errors. The set-off, of course, affected the shooting of the rifle, and had to be allowed for. The clumsy position of the sight was very apt to cause men to cant their rifles, and some used the left eye. Worse than all, perhaps, in trench warfare was the fact that with the Government pattern of telescopic sight, which was set on the side of the rifle, it was impossible to see through the loopholes of the steel plates which were issued, as these loopholes were naturally narrow; and looking into the tele-

First Army School of S.O.S. Comparison of sniper's robe as opposed to ordinary kit firing over a turnip heap. To find second sniper look for muzzle of rifle. Distance from camera, 8 yards.

scopic sight, when the muzzle of the rifle was pointing through the loophole, one got nothing but a fine view of the inside of the steel plate and the side of the loophole. Why the telescopic sights were set on the sides of the rifles was never definitely or satisfactorily explained, but it was always said that it was done so that rapid fire should be possible. I believe the decision was taken in the War Office, and if this is true, and the sight was set on the side for this reason (and one can see no other reason why it should have been so set) – then surely whoever was responsible can have had no knowledge whatever of the use of telescopic sights.

To take a telescopic sight off a rifle occupies not two seconds of time, and to think that a sniper could or would ever do rapid fire through a telescope sight, or need to load with a clip, shows nothing short of incredible ignorance. At any rate, the Germans made no such mistake, though they made many others.

Nevertheless, the sights came out to us in this form. By the time that representations had been made from high quarters in France asking that telescope sights should be set on top of the rifle, an alteration was impossible, as it would have thrown out all the factories who were engaged in the manufacture of these weapons. But once again, many a German owed his life to the original decision.

To take a concrete instance. One day I was down in the trenches and watching No Man's Land with a telescope. There was a sniper beside me who had one of my rifles, a Mauser, which had a telescope sight on the top, and with which he was able to fire through his loophole. It was very early in the morning, and the light had not strengthened, when a working party of Germans appeared who had been working under cover of some dead ground. They had but a few yards to go to regain their own trench. The sniper who was next to me got off a shot. Two of the snipers armed with the Government weapons a little farther along, who were waiting at loopholes, found that neither of them could bring their rifles to bear at the extreme angle at which the Germans were disappearing. Both ran out from their posts to try and get a shot over the top, but they were, of course, too late.

This is only one instance of a thing that was always happening. As we could not get the sights altered, the First Army and the 11th Corps arranged that their workshops should cut special sniping plates with large loopholes for the use of snipers armed with telescope sights. But even so it was always unsatisfactory, and the sight on the side of the rifle had a very circumscribed field of view when used from behind cover.

In order to show how little telescope sights were understood, it was, I think, in July 1916, that Lieutenant Colonel P W Richardson came out to France to lecture on telescopic sights. On his departure, he sent in a report to GHQ as to the inaccuracy of these sights. Colonel Richardson intended to draw attention only to the inaccuracy, for there is no man who is keener on these weapons or who knows their value better. The authority into whose hands the report fell read it quite differently, and a month or two afterwards there came down to Brigades, and indeed to all our formations, the question from GHQ as to whether it would not be well to abolish telescopic sights altogether, especially as "economy was now so urgent." The answers that went back to that question from GOC's were couched in no hesitating language, so that our telescope sights were not taken away. Had they been taken away, the German would once again have attained his sniping superiority, and

First Army School of S.O.S. Typical German Loophole Disguises in Earth Parapet

there would be many a man now alive and enjoying life who would never have left the endless series of trenches which we were yet destined to defend or capture.

But to get back to the course at the school. Our aim was to create good shots in as short a time as possible, and not only must they be good shots, but they must also be quick shots. After finding out errors in the ordinary way by grouping, we eschewed as far as possible shooting at targets; the round black bull on the white ground was very rarely used, and all kinds of marks were put up in its place. The head and shoulders was the most efficacious target, and practice was further carried on at dummy heads carried at walking pace along trenches. In fact, where such appliances as we had at the school are lacking, it is far better to allow snipers to shoot at tins stuck up on sticks than to permit them to become pottering target shots.

Speed was always the essence of sniping, and it was wonderful how, after short practice at the disappearing head, the men began to speed up. Competition was encouraged to the limit, and on every course a picked team of men shot against a picked team of officers. Those who were chosen for these matches were those who obtained the highest scores during the course. Further, a number of prizes were offered, and competition for these was always keen. Sometimes we had the Canadians and Colonials shooting against what they called the "Imperials," and sometimes the representatives of the Scottish regiments shot against the English.

One thing we always made a point of, and that was to take up every shooter to his target and show him exactly what he had done. A man with a telescope who spots each shot takes infinitely more interest in what he is doing than does a man who merely has results signalled to him, but going up to the target is the best method of all.

After eight days with the open sight, those who were considered worthy passed on to practise with the telescopic. One of our great difficulties was that the telescopic sights were so much wanted in the line that it was hard to call them away for courses; but, as a matter of fact, many battalions seemed to keep a telescopic sight, which they always sent on the course. It was generally a bad one, but this did not much matter, as we were continually having snipers sent up with the rifles they were actually using, in order that they might shoot them at the school. Thus a man might come on a course, and if he got a good report, might be back at the school within a week with a telescope sight, which he was thenceforward to use, and which we were asked to regulate to his hold.

But I do not want to go too far into this question of shooting, and it will not be necessary to say more than that of every hundred students who came to a course, somewhere about seventy-five went back as quite useful shots. We had many, of course, far above the class of "useful," and sometimes the competition for the champion shot of the classes was extraordinarily keen. Considering the very small bulls and the continually moving targets, the scores made at the school reflected great credit upon the students.

But though there was a great deal of shooting at the school, there were many other subjects also in which students were instructed. One of these was observation. The way that this was taught was exactly the same that I had used from the earliest days of 1915. Two trenches were dug at a distance of three or four hundred yards apart, and one of these trenches was an exact imitation of a piece of German line. Those who were to be taught observation were put with their telescopes and

There are two snipers here – one in uniform and one in a "sniper's robe".

notebooks in the other trench. A couple of scouts dressed in German uniforms showed themselves at certain points of the German trench and generally attempted to produce the exact happenings that would occur were those under instruction watching an actual piece of German line. Thus at one point of the trench earth would be thrown up, and five minutes later at another a man in a helmet carrying a pick would pass along. Here and there a loophole would be opened, and so on. The observation class kept a lookout upon the German trench, and noted down in their note books the time and place of all that happened therein, which they were able to observe. As far as possible, every member of the class was given a telescope of equal power, and it was an extraordinary thing to see how while some men sent in excellent reports, others seemed to be quite incapable of accurate observation.

Besides teaching the use of the telescope for front line work, this system gave a very useful practice lesson in the art of reporting things seen. Sometimes the officers of the staff or the Lovat Scouts attempted to crawl out of the German trench without being seen, and on one occasion two Lovat battle observers who were resting at the school crawled clean round an officer class unseen, and took them in the rear. This is an easy enough thing to do when the ground is favourable, but our trenches had been very carefully sited. There were at least three or four spots in which a man crawling was well within view, and in passing across these he had to exercise the most infinite care if he wished to obtain success.

At nighttime these two trenches were used for another purpose – that of teaching patrolling. Between them was a strip of typical No Man's Land with shell holes which we spent a whole day blowing up, wire, old uniforms – in fact, everything to make it as like the real thing as possible. After I left the school, Major Underhill had the bright idea of putting out in this No Man's Land a number of imitation German dead. In the pockets of these "dead" were *soldbuchs* – that is, the German paybooks – and various other identifications, which it is the duty of scouts to collect and send to HQ. I think there can be very little doubt that the conditions under which patrols worked and practised at First Army Sniping School approached the real in a very high degree. For instance, all our work was in competition, very often the officers against men, or Colonials against the World. Sometimes the defenders were supplied with pistols and Verey lights, which they fired off just as do the Germans. The attacking patrol carried with it small pegs with the patroller's name marked upon them. These pegs they stuck into the ground at the most advanced or important point, which they attained.

A certain amount of teaching of patrolling was done in the daytime by the use of night glasses. These were, the invention of Major Crum, of the King's Royal Rifles. On the sunniest day, once one had put on one of these pairs of goggles, one could not see more than was possible on the darkest night, and there is no doubt that a great deal was learnt by watching in daylight the kind of movements that a man must make at night.

Experience of scouting in No Man's Land showed that our patrols were most often spotted at the moment of leaving or returning to our own trenches. Great stress was laid on the proper way in which to get in and out of a trench. Another dangerous moment for the patrols was when they made a turning movement. The man who crept out with care and skill was apt to rise to his knees as he turned, and

A contrast showing the drawbacks of uniform and a "correct" position.

if a Verey light happened to be in the air at that moment, he was thus apt to give the whole show away.

There were many other subjects taught at the school into which I need not go, for those interested will find them all set out in the appendices, but special stress was always laid upon marching on compass bearings by night. It was an amazing thing how few officers really understood the prismatic compass, and indeed, how high a percentage of them did not possess a compass worth understanding. The advent of the gas mask, or box-respirator, added new difficulties to training, for it was necessary to carry out a good deal of our work under gas alarm conditions.

At least once on every course we had a scouting scheme. For this, the NCOs and men were told off in small parties, each under an officer, and were given a certain line to hold. They were to report all details of a military nature, which they saw, all transport, etc. Some of our staff scouts were sent out early in the day and were ordered to try and make their way back unseen through this line, and the staff instructors used to go out and see what they could of it. This scouting scheme gave great individual play to the fancy of the officer in charge of each party, and many of them used it to the full.

For some reasons, a story was started that I had once gone right along the road, which was the line that was being held, disguised as a French peasant. I had never done anything of the kind, but the keenness to spot me when I did go round was always a matter of amusement.

The training of observers at the school, as distinct from the front line telescope work, which I have described, was always extraordinarily interesting. I give in Appendix A the exact course the Lovat Scout reinforcement observers were put through. We were exceedingly lucky in having at the school so many first-rate glass-men, so that it was possible to get ahead with teaching the telescope very fairly quickly. Sometimes, through pure ignorance, a young observer, or an observer new to his work, would think he knew a great deal more than he actually did. It was only necessary to put him down for five minutes beside a Lovat Scout for him to rise a much wiser and less self-sufficient man!

Another branch of long-distance observation was the building of properly concealed observation posts, and by the time the school left Linghem, the plateau was honeycombed with posts looking in every direction.

Very early in the school's career, a model sniper's post was built, and all along one series of trenches we had model loopholes. One point that I always found when visiting the real trenches was that nearly all loopholes were made with three iron plates in the form of a box. This shape of loophole very much circumscribes the angle of fire. The true way to make a loophole is to set the two flanking plates at an angle of at least forty-five degrees, so that the field of fire may be enlarged.

One of the most important object lessons, which we used to have, was to send a sniper into the model trenches with orders to fire from different loopholes in turn. The rest of the class then watched the loopholes, and gave opinions as to which one the shot had come from. It takes a considerable amount of skill to fire from a loophole without giving away your position by the gas, which comes from your rifle muzzle. These demonstrations also taught the snipers how in the dry weather the dust round the mouth of a loophole will invariably give it away and how in cold weather the smoke will hang a little.

First Army School of S.O.S. Showing effects and importance of light and shade.

Lectures on aeroplane photographs were another side of our work, and one, which was undoubtedly very necessary. All the school trenches and, indeed, the whole school and plateau and the woods around it had been photographed from the air. Each officer or NCO student was provided with a photograph and went over the actual ground, Captain Kendall accompanying them to explain all details. In this way a practical knowledge of what trenches looked like from the air was gained.

The demonstrations showing the use of protective colouring and the choice of backgrounds always interested the classes very much. Often the whole class arrived within twenty yards of a man lying within full view without being able to spot him. On one occasion during a big demonstration, one of the staff was lying out in a coat of the colour and contour of sandbags on top of a trench, and the whole party of staff officers were all round him without having spotted his whereabouts. When I pointed him out a foreign officer who was present, and who evidently did not understand me, thought I was referring to an object a little further on, and in order to see it better he actually leaped on to the camouflaged man!

As a matter of fact, this protective colouration scheme business can very easily be overdone, for the man who lies out in the open is at the mercy of the changes of light and shade. What is an absolute protective background at eleven o'clock may become quite useless at twelve. But it was necessary to teach it to a certain extent, as in open warfare the observer and the scout have to obtain safety by concealment rather than by cover from fire.

Another of the most useful lessons at the school was undoubtedly the practical one of judging distance. On the average I think students were worse at distance judging than at any other subject, but a little practice made an enormous difference.

The ruling idea of the School was to make sniping as simple as possible, and for this purpose nothing was ever used in building a post or loophole, which could not be obtained at once in any trench in the British Army. There were many very elaborate loopholes, which could be indented for from the Special Works Park RE (Camouflage), but I do not think these were successful unless they were put in by specially selected officers. In sending indents to the Special Works Park, Commanding Officers usually forgot to mention the background and the kind of earth in which their trenches were dug.

A demonstration that used always to interest the class exceedingly was one which showed the effect of different forms of ammunition on various kinds of loophole plates, British and German. Some time in 1917 the Germans produced an armoured mask for snipers. This was of steel, and of great weight and thickness, and indeed it looked as if no bullet could possibly go through it, so much so that one of my officers volunteered to put it on and let someone have a shot at him. This I, of course, refused to countenance for a moment, and lucky it was, for the first shot went clean through the armoured headpiece. Anyhow, I should imagine, whether the shot pierced the visor or no, the man in it must almost certainly be stunned by a direct hit.

Although when first I became a sniping instructor, I used to have some firing practice at five and six hundred yards, when I went to the First Army School I gave this up. The chances of hitting a German head at six hundred yards with a telescope sight, if there is any wind blowing at all, are not great, for, as I have repeatedly said, a sighting shot is not possible. I came to the conclusion that continual popping away with telescopic-sighted rifles at six hundred yards simply wore out their barrels. After all, a rifle only lasts at its highest efficiency for, in certain cases, as few as five hundred rounds, and every shot taken through a telescope-sighted rifle shortens the life of the barrel. We, therefore, until warfare became more open, never went back further than four hundred yards, and our greatest difficulty was to teach the snipers to appreciate the strength of the wind. The system by which wind must be taught to snipers must be both very accurate and very simple, for some of the best snipers who came to the school had difficulty in making calculations. Usually we found that the best way to begin to teach wind allowance was to take the man up on the range, and for one of the staff to demonstrate against the stop butt. The class all had telescopes, and the puff of dust gave away the exact point at which the bullet struck. This system had the further advantage of teaching snipers what a distance of two feet looks like at three hundred yards. But individual practice is the only way to learn wind judging.

At the school we gave six different strengths of wind, gentle, moderate, fresh, strong, very strong, and gale, and it was, of course, in the judging of the gentle, moderate and fresh, that the difficulties lay. Our range had this advantage, that it was a good one on which to teach wind allowance by letting the men practise for themselves, for there was almost always a wind blowing.

Night firing and observation by moonlight, as well as many other schemes which the reader who is interested can see for himself in the curriculum which is set out in the appendix, took up the rest of our time; but, from the very earliest days, the moment the day's work was over we used to adjourn for games. At first we used to play rounders and baseball of a kind. Later we made a rough golf course of three or four holes. As soon as we got our Establishment and the school increased in size, games became a matter of great importance, and, as usual, football was by far the most popular. We had throughout a very good Association team, and sometimes were able to play two elevens on Saturday afternoons, and all the other days there were pick-up sides and punt-about.

In summer we played some cricket matches, and were never beaten, though once, one lovely summer evening, we adjourned for dinner at the end of our opponents' second innings having fifty runs to get to win. When we came out to get the fifty, it was so dark that we only pulled it off by one wicket.

In June, 1917, there was a conference of sniping officers at Boulogne, and here I first met the Commandants of the SOS Schools of the other armies: Lt-Col Sclater, DSO (2nd Army), Major Pemberthy (3rd Army), Major Michie, DSO (5th Army) and the Major commanding the School of the 4th Army. All the above are well known throughout the BEF for the splendid work they did.

One point which we always tried to impress on all who came to the school was the vital necessity for snipers and observers to take immediate action when anything unusual and not normal was seen. I give the following instance to illustrate this essential.

One day I had been ordered to visit a certain battalion in order to go round their sniping posts and to look over their telescope sights. As, through some mistake, their telescope sights were in the line, I had to use my own rifle to demonstrate with.

At this time I was shooting with a .350 Mauser, which, of course, carried special ammunition, and after the lecture, as there was still some light left, I wandered up to the line through the darkness of a large wood. Here there was a railway cutting, across which our trenches and those of the Germans opposing us lay. My batman was carrying my rifle, and I descended into this cutting, where we had a post. The Germans, at a distance of about 250 yards, had also a strong post across the cutting. Four or five privates were keeping a lookout upon the German line, but none of them had telescopes, and the moment I used mine I saw a German officer who was standing up and giving directions. I at once took my rifle only to find that my servant had left the cartridges behind.

Although I could see the German officer quite clearly through the telescope of the rifle, it was getting so dark that I could not pick him up with the open sights of one I borrowed, so that an accurate shot was out of the question; but with the telescope I was able to get an inkling of what he was doing. Very obviously, he was superintending the placing of a trench mortar into position with which to bombard the post in which I was; for I could see quite a movement of men, and earth was being continually thrown up.

It rapidly grew quite dark, and I went back and reported the matter to the proper authority. Now the proper authority was, I thought, not very much interested. Although I put the case very strongly, and said I was sure the *minenwerfer* would bombard our post next day, it appeared from subsequent events that he took no action, nor did he ring up the guns and ask them to demolish the German *minenwerfer* that night as I begged him to do. The result was that shortly afterwards our post was demolished, with loss of life.

There is no doubt that on that evening the star of the German officer was in the ascendant, for had I had a cartridge, the chances were enormously against his ever having left the trenches alive, as I had the range from the map and knew the shooting of my rifle to an inch.

Chapter Eight

Wilibald The Hun

[This and the following chapter are representative of the two sides of sniping – *ie* – shooting and observation. The incidents occurred.]

"Who've you got there?"

"Mr Harrison, sir; killed, sir."

A short, red-haired officer ranged up alongside the stretcher, turned back the blanket, and somewhat hurriedly replaced it.

"Damn those pointed bullets," he said, speaking in a detached kind of way and half to himself. His mind was working already on its problem.

"Where did it happen?"

"Caisson Trench, sir. That sniper Wilibald."

"When?"

"Just after nine, sir."

"Anyone with him?"

"Sergeant Small, sir."

The officer turned, and the stretcher party resumed its way. He stood watching them for a little, his thoughts roving from the horrible way in which a pointed bullet, fired from a rifle with a muzzle velocity of 3,000 feet a second, will at times keyhole, to the deeds and too-haunting personality of Wilibald the Hun. British troops have throughout the war given names to any German sniper whose deeds lent him a personality. Fritz is generic; but once let a Hun impress himself by skill, and he is christened. Thus we have known Adolfs, Wilhelms, Old Seventrees, Bluebeard, and a hundred others. At first, thanks to the Duke of Ratibor, who collected all the sportsmen's telescopic-sighted rifles in Germany – and it is proof of German far-sightedness that a vast percentage of them took the military cartridge – the Hun sniper took heavy toll against our blunt open sights. Later, things happened, and the plague was stayed; but, in the days of this incident, the Hun and the Briton were still striving unevenly for mastery.

The officer turned at length, and walked slowly down the trench till he came to company headquarters. A second lieutenant, standing at the entrance to the dugout, was unloading a rifle.

"Hullo, Bill," said the officer. "Whose rifle?"

"My batman's."

"What have you been doing with it?"

"Wilibald shot Jack Harrison through the head."

"I ..."

"Don't," said the red-haired officer shortly.

"Why not?"

"Have you ever shot with that rifle?"

"No."

The red-haired officer raised his eyes wearily.

"Wilibald's bag is big enough already. Wilibald sits over there" – he indicated the German position with a swinging movement – "in some hole or other as snug as a bug in a rug, with a telescope sighted rifle which he knows to the inch. You go and look for him with a rifle you don't know to a yard. You … fool!"

"All right, Red. We know your hobby. Only we wish you'd deliver the goods."

"Meaning Wilibald?"

"Yes. Wilibald is becoming a public nuisance. He's got nine of us, including an officer and an NCO, and he's got more than a dozen of the West Blanks who relieve us. He's … Damn! That's him."

A shot had rung out, followed by an ejaculation. The two officers hurried along the trench to where in a bay a consequential private was pouring iodine into a sergeant's cheek. Three or four other privates were talking excitedly.

"It come from the 'Un trench."

"It didn't. It come from the trees in the spinney."

"That's right. The fifth tree."

"Naw. The sixth."

"Garn!"

Red, with a word, broke up the group, and addressed the sergeant:

"Hullo, Small. What's happened?"

"I was takin' a spy, and Wilibald 'ad a drive at me. Clipped my cheek, 'e did," said Small, in the aggrieved voice of the NCO whose dignity has been touched.

"Then, for God's sake, don't take a spy, Small, until you learn how to do it without offering a target. 'Let's see your cheek. Only a scratch. That's lucky. Now, did you see where the shot was fired from?"

"Beyond that it come from the left flank, I did not, sir. I …"

"All right. Go and get your cheek bandaged."

As the sergeant saluted and went off down the trench, Red, having ordered the observers to keep a good look-out upon the enemy trench, took off his cap, and, fixing it on his stick, told Bill to raise it slightly above the parapet until the badge of a famous regiment glinted in the sun, while he watched.

Nothing happened.

Red laughed.

"Wilibald's not a dasher," said he. "He's a regular Hun. Probably has some rule about not firing unless he can see half the head he's aiming at. 'Shoot to kill' is his motto. Useful man, Wilibald, I wonder if his company commander appreciates him."

After passing along the trench and warning its garrison not to give unnecessary targets, Red went a round of his observers. They were stationed at loopholes and in OPs.

"Keep a good look-out, and try to spot Wilibald if he fires again. The light will be pretty good when the sun works round behind us."

"Which part of the trench do you think he is in, sir?" asked a lance corporal.

"Don't know; perhaps not in the trench at all. Some of the Royalshires thought he was in the spinney, and some thought he was in the willow trees. He got twelve of them. He must be dealt with."

"Yes, sir," said the lance corporal optimistically.

It was four o'clock in the afternoon when Red, having passed down an old disused trench in the rear of the British position, crawled cautiously out behind the parados. Here was an area seamed with shell holes, each half-full of green, scummy water, little piles of rotting sandbags, rusty wire, nettles, and coarse grass. About fifty yards behind the front line, a heavy shell had fallen almost on the top of the almost imperceptible rise which culminated at that point. This shell hole was Red's objective, for from it he could, he knew, get a fair view of the German trenches. It was not a safe place to visit in the morning, when the sun was behind the German lines, and everything in the British stood out clearly to their Zeiss glasses; but in the afternoon the position was reversed, and the Hun observers were in their turn looking into the sun.

To this place Red made his way. It was long before the days of snipers' robes of canvas, painted yellow and green and black, which for such work would have been useful, though the earlier patterns, cut like a greatcoat, were difficult to crawl in. Later a pattern of overall shape was issued, which gave free play to the knees; but, as we say, such issues were not yet "available."

At length, Red reached the shell hole and slowly made a place for his telescope among the clods of earth upon the crater-lip. Then he bent himself to a careful study of the scene.

The line of the German trenches was marked in white, for it was a somewhat chalky country, with here and there loophole plates sticking gauntly up on the top of the parapet. To these Red gave no attention. Many of them were dummies; the danger-spots, he knew, were set lower; often upon the ground level, where, through some gap in the rusty wire, the German sniper's eyes watched ceaselessly for a "target." Very carefully Red examined the German trenches. Well he knew their appearance. One by one he picked up the familiar landmarks; here a machine-gun emplacement, there a suspected sniper's post. All was quiet. Once a sentry fired, and the bullet hummed like a bee high above him. Next, Red turned more to the business in hand – the location of Wilibald. No easy business, since there was a great divergence of opinion. He had been located so often, in a sniping-post by the black sandbags – for at one point in the Hun trenches there were a number of black sandbags; the Germans used all colours on that front. Red turned his glass on that point. Yes, there seemed to be a post there, but there was nothing to prove that it was tenanted. Then he tried the spinney; but neither the third tree nor the fifth yielded up any secret. Then the ruined house or hovel; after that, the wide expanse of No Man's Land. As he watched, Red remembered the words of the Corps Commander: "There is no No Man's Land. It must be our land right up to the enemy trenches." That was an ideal to live up to. But stare now as he would, and as he continued to do for an hour, he saw nothing, could see nothing of Wilibald. Broken wire, shell holes, sandbags, pulverized bricks and mortar, men lying in queer positions, men whose ragged tunics the evening wind stirred strangely, men who would never move again,

All Red's life he had been apt, in moments of tension, to recur to a phrase which made a kind of background to his thoughts, and now he found himself repeating:

"Exiled and in sorrow far from the Argive Land."

He turned round and glanced at the sun. it was sinking red, like a cannon ball. Then he turned for a last look at No Man's Land and the Hun positions. Nothing stirred. Far away on the right, a mile or two away, a machine-gun sounded like a rapidly worked typewriter. A bat flew and turned above the British trench fifty yards in front of him. Red crawled back.

In the trench he met his brother officer Bill.

"Hullo, Red. Any luck?"

"No."

Bill laughed.

"Wilibald's some man."

Red nodded.

That evening at mess Wilibald formed the topic of conversation. The Colonel spoke of him very seriously.

"He must be a splendid shot," said he. "He puts it through the loophole in the post in Bay 16, two shots in three – at least, so Carpenter, of the Blankshires, was telling me. Said he supposed he'd got one of those big Zeiss telescopic sights which magnify four times. Shooting with 'em must be as easy as falling off a log."

"Yes, sir," said Red.

It was a full hour before dawn that the chill woke Red in his dugout. His thoughts switched at once on to the subject of Wilibald. The man had taken over twenty British lives. He pictured him waiting at his loophole, his bearded cheek pressed to the stock of his rifle. A fine shot, no doubt – Carpenter had said that he put two shots out of three into the loophole of Bay 16 sniping-post ... Good shooting. Dashed good. It was cold, though! The first cold morning. By Jove!

Red had an idea. He rose and dressed hastily, his dressing consisting of little but pulling on his boots and tunic. He took his telescope and made his way along the dark trench until he came to Bay 16. A figure was leaning against the side of the post. Red realized that it was Corporal Hogg, a NCO of sound sense.

"Corporal!"

"Yes, sir!"

"Anyone in the Post?"

"No, sir. You told me not to have it manned at night, lest the flash should give it away."

"Quite right. Now listen. I want the loophole shut. As soon as it is light enough to shoot – at 5.15 say – I want you to open it cautiously. Open it from the side, in case Wilibald – got that?"

"Yes, sir."

"Understand. Loophole to be closed till 5.15 a.m. Then to be opened by you cautiously, and from one side. I shall be out in the shell hole behind the parados."

Half an hour later Red crouched in the shell hole, his telescope discarded, since its field of view was too narrow. In front of him lay his watch, which he had synchronized with that of Corporal Hogg. The hand marked 5.11. The moments passed. Red's heart was beating now. He glanced – a last glance, a very hurried glance – at his watch. It was past the fourteen minutes! Hogg would. be opening the loophole.

Bang!

A shot had rung out. From the garden – or what was once the garden – of the razed house, not seventy yards distant, a little wisp of gas floated away to the cold morning star. Very cautiously Red wrapped a bit of sandbag round his telescope, and pushed it on the little plot of turnips.

At first he saw nothing.

Then he was aware of some turnip-tops moving, when all the rest were still. A moment later he had made out the top of Wilibald's head, garlanded with turnip-tops, and the upper part of Wilibald's large German face. This, then, was the explanation of the accurate shooting and the long death roll. Wilibald had been firing at short range.

Red felt it was almost uncanny.

Hitherto, in trench warfare, as far as daylight was concerned, the Huns had seemed to him almost an abstraction, creatures apparent to the sense of hearing certainly, but troglodytes who popped above ground for only a passing moment, and then only to disappear. But this man, not one hundred yards away ...

Red withdrew into the shell hole and quickly mapped out his course. He must at once get back to his own trench. To do so meant a crawl over what must be the skyline to Wilibald, and consequently a point Red could hardly hope to pass unobserved. Red marked a thistle. It was there that he would come into view. He would remain so for about ten yards. Of course, could he once regain his own trench he could take steps to deal with Wilibald, but at present the Hun held the better cards. Red smiled grimly when he thought of his crawl to the shell hole of the previous evening.

To the sun, which was shining straight into Wilibald's eyes, he most certainly owed his life. Now that sun was behind Wilibald ... Red started. As he neared the thistle, his heart beat fast and quick. He passed the thistle. He felt very like a fly crawling over an inverted plate while someone with a flytrap waited to strike. He was crawling straight away now. The thistle was behind him. Another four yards – two – one– still Wilibald did not fire, and, with a deep sigh of relief, Red hurled himself into the disused sap and safety.

Later the CO was speaking.

"So Wilibald's gone west?"

"Yes, sir."

"How did you spot him?"

"The cold woke me. I have noticed how the gas from a rifle hangs on chilly days. Wilibald forgot that. He had a shot at the loophole of No 16 Bay Post, and I was watching, and spotted him. He was lying out in the turnips, about seventy yards from our line. He had turnip-tops fixed round his cap, and lay in a hole he'd dug. He must have come out before dawn and gone back after dark. He was a pretty gallant fellow, sir."

The CO nodded.

"D-d gallant," said he.

"I thought, sir, if you'd no objection, I'd take a patrol out and fetch him in – for purposes of identification."

So Wilibald was brought in. His cap, some letters in his pocket, and his shoulder-straps were forwarded to Brigade; but his rifle, beautifully fitted with a Zeiss telescope sight, which had taken over twenty British lives, turned its muzzle east instead of west, and began to take German lives instead.

Chapter Nine

The Cat

I

The two snipers of the Royal Midlandshires, the shooter and the observer, were comfortably in their post. The shooter was longing for a cigarette, which regulations forbade lest the enemy – two hundred yards away – should see the smoke issuing from the concealed loophole; but the observer, Private William. Entworth, was studying the parapet opposite.

Suddenly he spoke:

"Line of water-tower. Red sandbag. Left. Two feet."

Saunders' eyes picked up the water tower in the distance, ranged to the parapet, found the red sandbag, and then swung to the left of it. Yes, something moving. He cuddled the stock of his rifle, and brought the pointer in the telescope to bear. Then slowly he began to squeeze the trigger.

"Don't shoot."

Entworth was only just in time.

"Why not, ole son?"

"It's only a cat."

"A 'Un cat! 'Ere goes."

"Come off it. If you get shootin' cats outer this post Mr Nowell'll ... Besides, it's rather a nice lookin' cat. Tortoiseshell colour. We 'ad one in Ferrers Street 'e reminds me of ... There, 'e's climbin' up on the bloomin' parados, curlin' round and goin' to sleep just as if there wasn't no war. Shall I enter 'im?"

"Wot's the good?"

"Dunno. Shows we was awake. 'Time 11.25 Ac. Emma. Cat (tortoiseshell) at K22.C.35.45. Action taken: None.'"

So wrote Private Entworth with laborious pencil. As he finished a voice sounded outside.

"Who's in there?"

"Private Entworth. Private Saunders."

"Shut the loopholes. I am coming in."

"Well, seen anything?" questioned Mr Nowell, the Sniping and Intelligence Officer of the Battalion.

"They've been working on the post at K.22. D.85.60."

"Seen any Huns?"

"Only a cat, sir. I've entered it in the logbook. It's sunning itself on the parados now, sir. Line of water tower. Red sandbag."

"Yes, I have it," said Nowell, who had taken the telescope.

"Shall I shoot 'im, sir?"

"Why should you?"

"'E probably kills rats and makes life brighter like for the 'Un, sir, by so doing. There's a glut o' rats on this sector, sir."

99

"The cat looks very comfortable. No, don't shoot, Saunders. Entworth, give me that log-book."

The officer turned over the pages.

"I wonder if anyone has ever seen that cat before? Hullo, yes. Private Scroggins and Lance-Corporal Tew two days ago in the afternoon. Here's the entry: '3.4 pip emma K.22.C.35.40. Cat on parados.'"

Howell's eyes showed a gleam of interest.

"Note down whenever you see that cat," said he.

"Yes, sir."

"And keep a bright look-out."

"Yes, sir."

Once more the loopholes were shut, and Nowell, lifting the curtain at the back of the Post which prevented the light shining through, went out.

His steps died away along the trench-boards.

"Think we'll see it in 'Comic Cuts'?" (the universal BEF name for the Corps Intelligence Summary). "'At K.22.C.35.45, a tortoiseshell-coloured he cat.' I don't think!" said Saunders.

"Shouldn't wonder. The cove wot writes out 'Comic Cuts' must 'a bin wounded in the 'ed early on. Sort o' balmy 'e is."

II

Meantime we must follow Mr Nowell down the trench. He was full of his thoughts and almost collided round a corner with a red-hatted Captain.

"Sorry, sir," said he, saluting.

"Righto! my mistake. Can you tell me where I shall find the ISO of this battalion?" asked the Staff Officer.

"My name's Nowell, sir. I am the Sniping and Intelligence Officer."

"Good. I'm Cumberland of Corps Intelligence."

Nowell looked up with new interest. He had heard of Cumberland as a man of push and go, who had made things hum since he had come to the Corps a few weeks back.

"Anything you want?" continued Cumberland. "You've been sending through some useful stuff. I thought I'd come down and have a talk."

Nowell led the way to his dugout. He had suffered long from a very official Corps Intelligence GSO, whom Cumberland had just replaced. Under the old regime, it never really seemed to matter to the Higher Intelligence what anyone in the battalion did, but now Cumberland seemed to take an interest at once. After a quarter of an hour's talk Cumberland was taking his leave.

"Well," said he, "anything you want from Corps, don't hesitate to ask. That's what we're there for, you know. Sure there isn't anything?"

"As a matter of fact there is, but I hardly like to ask you."

"Why not?"

"It's such a long shot, sir."

"Well, what is it?"

"I'd like aeroplane photos taken of K.22 squares C and D opposite here. New photographs, sir."

Cumberland was about to ask a question, but looking up he caught the slight flush of colour that had risen in Nowell's face.

"Righto," he said easily. "We rather pride ourselves on quick work with aeroplane photos up at Corps. I'll have the squares taken tomorrow morning if visibility is *pukka*. And the finished photos will be in your hands by five o'clock. Good afternoon."

Cumberland strode along the trench, and Nowell stood staring after him.

"Never asked me what I wanted 'em for," he muttered. "Taken in the morning; in my hands by afternoon. Why, in old Baxter's time such efficiency would have killed him of heart disease. Well, let's hope that cat's playing the game and not leading a poor forlorn British Battalion Intelligence Officer to make a fool of himself."

III

The next afternoon the aeroplane photos duly arrived, together with a note from Cumberland:

Dear Nowell,

Am sending the photographs of K.22.C and D taken today, also some I have looked out of the same squares which were taken six weeks ago. It would appear from a comparison that a good deal of work has been put in by the Hun round C.3.5. It looks like a biggish HQ. I have informed CRA who says it will be dealt with at 3 pip emma tomorrow, 18th inst.

C CUMBEIRLAND,
Captain GS.

IV

It is five minutes to three on the following day, and the bright sun which has shone all the morning has worked round behind the British position.

In the morning two gunner FOO's have visited the trenches, compared certain notes with Mr Nowell, and gone back to their Observation Posts on the higher ground. Nowell himself has decided to watch events from the OP in which was laid the first scene of this history. He hurries along to it, and calls out:

"Who's in there?"

"Private Saunders. Private Entworth, sir."

"Shut the loopholes. I'm coming in."

He goes in.

"Move along, Entworth, and I'll sit beside you on the bench and observe with my own glass. Get yours on to the spot where the cat was. Got it? Right. Two batteries of 6-inch Howitzers are going to try and kill that cat, Entworth, in a minute and a half from now. Zero at three o'clock. Nice light., isn't it?"

At these words of Nowell's, several thoughts, mostly connected with his officer's sanity, flashed through Entworth's rather slow brain, but long before they were formulated Nowell rapped out:

"Here they come."

Sounds just like half a dozen gigantic strips of silk being torn right across the sky were clearly audible in the Post. At the same instant through the watching glasses heaps of earth, tin, a stovepipe, were hurled into the air. There were other grimmer objects, too, as the shells rained down.

Fifteen minutes later, Mr Nowell having gone, Private Entworth was speaking, though his eye was still glued to his glass.

"Direct 'it right off *and* right into a nest of 'Uns. There was 'ole 'Uns and bits of 'Uns in the air, I tell yer, Jim Saunders. Loverly shooting, 'twas!. I doubt there's anything at C.35.45. left alive. There is, tho'! By … there is! There goes that ruddy coloured cat over the parados like a streak, and what 'o! for Martinpunch!"

V

And finally an extract from "Comic Cuts," the Corps Intelligence Summary of the next day:

"A cat having been observed by our snipers daily sleeping on the parados of a supposedly disused enemy trench at K.22.C.3.4. it was deduced from the regularity of its habits that the cat lived nearby, and – owing to the fact that the German trenches at this point are infested by rats – probably in a dugout occupied by enemy officers. Aeroplane photographs were taken which disclosed the existence of a hitherto unlocated enemy HQ, which was duly dealt with by our Artillery."

Chapter Ten

The Training of the Portuguese

When first we saw the Portuguese troops upon the roads of France, we did not dream that it would fall to our lot to train them in sniping, scouting and observation. But it did so fall, and after one or two Portuguese officers had been attached to the school for instruction, we were suddenly ordered to take an entire Portuguese class. This was the first of three or four, and we usually had eight officers and forty NCOs and men at a time.

The Portuguese were equipped largely, as is known, by the British, and had served out to them our short service rifle. In the Portuguese Army they use the Mauser, so our rifle was new to all ranks, and had to be carefully explained.

Of course, the great difficulty in training Portuguese troops lay in the necessity for the use of interpreters. One of my NCOs was able to talk Portuguese, which was of great assistance, and from time to time an English-speaking Portuguese officer was attached; but for the most part none of the officers and men who came to the school could speak a word of English, and the result, as I say, was that we had to carry on through interpreters.

In one of the first classes there was a Portuguese sergeant who was extremely capable and very keen on his work. As a mark of appreciation, I gave this sergeant, when he went away, a very nice telescope. About three weeks later the sergeant, who had spent the intervening time in the trenches, turned up at the school and said that he wished to speak to the Commandant. He said that he had come to thank me again for the telescope, as it had enabled him to spot a concentration of some fifty Germans, on to whom he had successfully directed artillery fire. He had taken the trouble to walk out quite a number of miles – at least ten or twelve – to inform me of his success. Poor fellow, he was afterwards badly gassed, and when I last saw him was in a very bad way. He was a most useful man as an observer, as he had been the master of some small coasting craft, which used to sail up and down the coast between Lisbon and Setubal and had knowledge of instruments.

Considering that the Portuguese troops did not know anything about our rifle, they really came along very quickly in shooting. One of the classes was at the school when we were informed that the Portuguese Corps Commander and Staff and various British GSO's would come over to see a "demonstration" two days before the course ended. The demonstration included shooting at dummy heads exposed for four seconds – five rounds; application on a 6-inch bulls-eye at two hundred yards; an attack upon a position; and a demonstration of the work of scouts. As soon as the Portuguese troops realized that they were to be inspected at the end of the course, there was a tremendous competition among them to get into the shooting team, and when the day arrived the eight who were picked obtained 34 hits out of 40 shots on the dummy head. At the 200 yards application the team scored 208 out of a possible 224. This shows how quickly shooting can be taught when both men and instructors are all out for success.

The greatest difficulty we had was training Portuguese as observers. None of them had used a telescope before, and it was very difficult to make them realize its possibilities. Of course, I am here talking of the private soldiers. The officers in their observation often made excellent reports and developed the greatest keenness on the work. There was one thing which occurred, owing to my attempting to speak Portuguese myself, which always struck me as not without its humorous side.

I had been attempting to point out to a squad of Portuguese scouts the elementary fact that when you were looking through a bush, or through roots or grass, it was sometimes well worthwhile to put a leaf or two into your cap. I sent them off to do this, keeping with me a few of their number to observe the value of the experiment. The rest went over the brow of the hill and were away for some period of time, so long that I was just going to see what was happening when suddenly a bush, followed by several other trees, began to move slowly over the hill! I found that the squad, not quite understanding my instructions, had cut down small trees with their large knives, had bound them upon their backs, and in the shadow of these were advancing upon me!

A part of their training upon which the Portuguese were extraordinarily keen was patrolling in No Man's Land. Usually at the school we used to begin this as soon as it was dark, often in summer, therefore, as late as eleven o'clock at night. After two or three hours' patrolling the Portuguese always still wanted to continue, and once they got out into our large imitation No Man's Land it was not easy to get them back again.

At one time, when we had a class of Portuguese, to whom we had been teaching patrolling, an officer and sergeant, who were making a round of Sniping and Infantry Schools, to give demonstrations on patrolling, turned up at the school. The Portuguese held the trench while the demonstrators set out to show them the way in which a reconnaissance patrol should be conducted. I was lying beside the Portuguese trench, and at once realized that something was afoot. Presently one of the Portuguese officers came up, and said, "Our men say that they hear them and can capture them." I told them to go ahead and do it.

Well, that patrol developed. A battle was going on at the time in the north, and all the plateau was lit with the flashes of the guns and the flares of the Verey lights, which the Germans kept firing into the air. For a long time there was silence. The Portuguese, who had had several days at the school and were learning well, had sent out a strong patrol, which very skilfully worked round and surrounded the hostile reconnaissance. I do not know what happened in No Man's Land, but the sergeant who was doing the demonstration, and who was a jujitsu expert, famous in pre-war days in the music halls, was captured and carried in by the Portuguese. There must have been a considerable scrap, for the sergeant was too stiff to come on parade next day! The Portuguese were much pleased at their success, and almost immediately afterwards they went back to the line, where a German patrol of eleven came out against them. The Portuguese tried their surrounding tactics with such success that they killed eight and captured three.

One day I was asked by the Portuguese Corps commander to attend a review of the Portuguese Army, which was being held at Marthes, some six miles from my Headquarters. When the time for the march past came, I saw the forty observers we had trained go by under their officers as a separate unit, each with a large white "O" sewn upon his sleeve.

The great difficulty was to obtain telescopes for these observers, for the demand was, all through the war, vastly in excess of the supply. The GS (General Service) telescope used by signallers in the British Army was, I believe, afterwards issued to the Portuguese troops, and this was a quite good enough glass for the purpose.

Another part of our training which the Portuguese troops took with enthusiasm was the physical training and jujitsu.

Sometimes when we had mixed classes, it was very difficult indeed, as all lectures had to be repeated in Portuguese. The ordinary daily morning talks on the care and cleaning of the rifle, the stalking telescope, or on the work of snipers in attack and defence, which usually took from thirty to forty minutes, used to tail out, as each sentence was translated, into a matter of an hour and a half and even two hours.

But I think that, on the whole, the Portuguese troops really enjoyed their time at the school, and I remember our taking the field at Association football with a good sprinkling of them in our team.

Chapter Eleven

The Modern Scout

In all previous wars, the scouts and patrols have had their own special place. In this, the greatest of all wars, although there was much scouting done – far more than in any previous war – yet in many respects it was of so different a nature that a new era in these practices may fairly be said to have set in.

In former wars, the individual scout had far more chance. In the Boer War, for instance, Major F R Burnham, DSO, an American who held a commission in the British Army, made a wonderful name for himself, as did Dan Theron on the Boer side.

First and last, I suppose that Burnham was the greatest scout of our time. Physically a small man, he was amazingly well knit, and very strong, and his many feats of hardihood owed much to his compact and untiring build. His name will live on account of two feats – the first, his passing through the entire Matabele Army and shooting the M'limo, the witch doctor, who was responsible for the Matabele War; and the second, his dash through the Boer lines, when he blew up the railway on the far side of Pretoria.

The first article of Burnham's faith was absolute physical fitness, and his idea of physical fitness was much more rigorous than that of most athletes. It was not with him a matter of merely keeping his muscles of speed and endurance in good fettle, but – what is a much harder thing – the keeping of all his senses at their highest pitch of efficiency. Thus, apart from his hearing, and eyesight, which were very keen, I have never met anyone else, except one Indian, who possessed anything like his sense of smell. He could smell a small fire in the open at an extraordinary distance, and he told me that this power had often been of the greatest value to him.

But Burnham was essentially, as a scout, the product of what may be called a savage, or extra-European War, and in this war there was no one on either side who had anything like the same opportunities of hand-to-hand work. Whereas it would perhaps be too much to say that the day of Burnham has passed forever, yet it is true enough that a new generation of scouts has arisen, whose work, or much of it, has been of a very different nature. In open or semi-open warfare a scout may still be ordered to go by day or night, and find out if this or that village is occupied by the enemy, but once trench warfare sets in, and the battle fronts of the opposing armies stretch from the sea to Switzerland, the work of the scout undergoes great changes. His theatre of action is No Man's Land, which comprises all the area between the two armies, which are drawn up one against the other.

The Corps Commander of the 11th Corps, Sir R Haking, would never allow the use of the word "No Man's Land." "There is no such place opposite my Corps," he would say. "All the land right up to the edge of the enemy's parapet is our land, and we have got to have control of it."

I believe I am right in stating that about seven out of every ten raids undertaken on the First Army Front in 1916 were the work of the 11th Corps, and they had long held the record in the number of prisoners taken in a single raid.

The work of the scout was, of course, to dominate the enemy in No Man's Land, and to this end he was continually patrolling it during the hours of darkness. Little, as a rule, is done by daylight, though Gaythorne-Hardy, who was Intelligence Officer of the 4th Battalion of the Royal Berkshire Regiment, and whom I have referred to before, in order to investigate the German wire under Hill 63, near Messines, decided, after looking at the ground with a telescope, to crawl out by day. The German lines were some three to four hundred yards away. The season was summer, and the grass long. In winter, crawling between the lines was almost impossible, owing to lack of cover.

The officer in question, accompanied by a corporal, crawled right up to the enemy wire, and got all information and a complete plan of the ground and obstacles. It was a task upon which any but a skilled hunter of big game, as my friend is, might easily have given himself away. To crawl across three hundred yards of open ground, with hundreds of German eyes watching for any movement, and bent on investigating any suspicious spot with a machine-gun, calls for courage and good nerve. This officer, however, had examined his route, decided to make the attempt, and he came back successful. He said it was no more difficult than stalking a deer. He was awarded the Military Cross, and the corporal is now a sergeant with the DCM.

But not much was done in No Man's Land in daylight. Snipers lay out in it, and sentries watched it, and both sides sent a deal of lead across it, but when night fell, it became, tenanted, and scouts and patrols crawled out into it – and sometimes never came back. The aim, of course, was always domination, and in order to gain domination many strange things were done.

For instance, there was the "Silent Death," as it was called, invented by the Canadians, who, under cover of darkness, crawled out into No Man's Land every night and lay there awaiting the advent of a German patrol. If such came, it was attacked hand to hand with trench daggers, and its members killed as silently as possible. This soon made the Germans very shy of taking their evening crawl, when so many of them who had gone over the top vanished into the darkness and were never heard of again.

At length the Germans almost gave up patrolling in that sector, and one of my officers who used to be in charge of a "Silent Death" party has often told me how dull and chilly were those long and weary waits in the frost or the rain, waiting for Huns who never came.

In trench warfare, No Man's Land was the cockpit of the war. Some sections of it were more favourable than others for action, but every evening and every night a great number of British used to go out in front. When one first went out, it seemed almost certain that one must be killed. There was a spasmodic sputter of fire from machine-guns, but as an actual matter of fact, moving about in No Man's Land was much safer than it seemed.

At first our patrols were very haphazard, and you could sometimes hear a private roaring out that a patrol was out, and that it would return at such and such an hour to such and such a point. This was giving away things with a vengeance to any

Night-work in No Man's Land (from a drawing by Ernest Blaikley)

Germans who spoke English, and it sounds almost impossible that it should have been done yet it was done, and not in isolated cases only.

I do not think that scouts ever got very far into the German lines, at any rate, during the continuance of trench warfare. To do so was well nigh impossible, and behind the German battlefront the place of the scout was taken by the spy or secret service agent.

But to return to No Man's Land. There was a certain sergeant who got a DCM for removing a trench board. A raid was projected by us, and, as usual, a careful rehearsal had been gone through. The scheme was to attack a certain sector of enemy trenches about two hundred yards long. This length of trench had to be blocked off at each end, so as to prevent assistance coming to the enemy down the trench from either flank.

Two parties were therefore told off to capture and hold the two points, which were to be the limits of our raid. Both parties went over, the northern party arriving in strength, but the southern had casualties from machine-gun fire, and finally only the sergeant and one private arrived in the enemy trench. Here the private was killed before the enemy fled, and there was only the sergeant to form the block and keep off the reinforcements, which were sure to come.

The sergeant, however, was a man of resource, and he swiftly removed the duck-board from the trench draining well – a large sump hole, or pit, which lay between him and the path taken by the retreating Germans. The trenches are often drained by pits of this kind, dug in the middle of the right-of-way, and bridged by a duckboard laid across them. In these pits there collected a mass of liquid mud as thick as glue. The sergeant removed the duckboard, and re-laid it eight or ten feet on his side of the mud-hole. Then he went round the corner of the next traverse, and waited to see what would happen.

Meantime, the main raiding party had got to work, and soon enemy reinforcements came rushing along the trench towards the sergeant. Seeing the duckboard ahead of them, they mistook the position of the mud-hole, and in they crashed. Soon the hole was as full of men as is a newly opened tin of sardines. Next the sergeant opened fire upon them. The whole raid was a glorious success. Prisoners were taken, and German dug-outs blown up – a result that could hardly have occurred had it not been that the sergeant had the sense and acumen to remove the duckboard, thus, by a very simple action, holding up quite a mass of reinforcements.

There is another raid story, for which I do not vouch, but which was firmly believed in the First Army.

All enemy movement was watched by aeroplanes, and photographed and reported. As the war went on, the science of aeroplane photography, progressed enormously. It is hardly too much to say that the Germans could not deepen a trench without our knowing it almost at once. We never made a raid – or, at least, need never have made one – without all who were going over, even down to the private soldier, having the opportunity of studying photographs of the trenches where their work lay.

The Germans, of course, did the same, but in a limited degree, as their aeroplanes did not dare to come over our lines in the way that ours crossed theirs.

Once, when the Germans were contemplating a raid, their Flying Corps succeeded in taking photographs of that portion of our trenches which was to be attacked. With the help of these photographs, the German Command caused to be built an exact replica of the trenches, which they intended to raid. They did this at no great distance behind their lines, with a view to rehearsing the raid just as a play is rehearsed in a theatre. We, of course, often did the same.

But to continue. One of our aeroplanes happened to pass over just as the Germans were having a daylight rehearsal, and, noticing the concentration of troops and the new workings of earth, a photograph was taken. This photograph was, of course, sent in the ordinary routine to Army Headquarters.

The Army possessed an extremely capable aerial photography expert, who soon made his deduction, and as he, of course, possessed the photographs of the entire front line system of the Army, it was not long before he had identified that piece of it which the Germans had copied and on which they were meditating an attack.

There was only one object, which could lead them to practise attacks upon so short a length of line. A raid was clearly in contemplation. The expert informed the General Staff of his discovery, and the General Staff informed those who were manning the threatened area. Preparations were made and precautions taken, and, sure enough, the Germans came over, to meet about as hot a reception as even modern war can provide.

As I say, I do not know if this story is apocryphal or not, but if it is, others about our aeroplane photography and its amazing efficiency were common talk in the Army.

Psychologically, going out into No Man's Land in the dark, especially if you are alone, is a distinctly eerie business. I really have no right to write much about it, as I was only out in front on a few occasions. On one, I remember, I was more frightened than I hope ever to be again. Although the story is personal, as it is against myself there can be no harm in telling it.

I had gone out to a cottage, which stood in No Man's Land. It was pretty dark, and a wild night, and there was, of course, a chance that some German might be in the cottage, which, though heavily shelled, was not entirely smashed.

After listening for a while and hearing no sound, I went in, and on the ground floor there was nothing but the usual mass of rubble and brick. A ladder led up to the second floor, and I climbed up this and began to tiptoe across the floor. One got a good deal of light from the star-shells which were thrown up by the Germans, but in a particularly dark moment I suddenly felt my left leg go from under me. I thought that it had been plucked away by some crouching Hun, or else that I had been hit by some missile – in fact, never did thoughts come quicker or more confusedly! What had really happened was that I had put my leg through the floor, and had got rather a heavy jar. But anything more disagreeable than that moment I have never experienced.

Of course, it is only one of the little incidents that are the hourly lot of those who go out into No Man's Land, but one's nerves are on these occasions strung up to a very high pitch.

But, as I say, my experience of No Man's Land was really so small as to be negligible, for when I was in the line I was sniping or observing all day, and you cannot do that and work at night also.

Crawling out into No Man's Land in daylight is a very different business, and if there is reasonable cover, it is to my mind more satisfactory to crawl out then, when your life depends on your own skill, than to crawl about in the dark over the bodies of men who have been dead for weeks, and when Chance of the blindest kind absolutely rules the game.

Now, of course, when a patrol is sent out, the report handed in should be in a definite and generally accepted form, giving the composition of the patrol.

I can perhaps explain my meaning best by referring the reader to the appendix on Patrols, at the end of this book.

Of course, patrolling in No Man's Land is only one small part of a scout's duties, and when the war became more open, there were many opportunities for scouts.

One point that struck me as being exceedingly valuable was the proper delivery of messages by runners. Major Crum used to demonstrate this by a small piece of acting, which was extraordinarily well done, in which an object lesson was given as to how not to deliver a message, and how a message should be delivered. In moments of excitement many men become somewhat prolix, and it is of the utmost importance that they should be taught to get their message into the fewest and clearest possible words.

A question that arose as the war went on was the definition of the duties of a sniper and a scout. It was held in some quarters that a sniper and a scout were two quite different men, who had in view two entirely different objects. The sniper, those who held this view said, was a man whose first duty was offensive action against the enemy, whereas a scout's duty was not to fight, but to obtain information. We at the school could never see it in this light, for there must be occasions when a scout must fight to get his information back, or indeed, to obtain it, and it seemed futile that in the morning a man should ask himself, "Am I today a sniper or a scout?"

I would not refer to these opinions had they not been rather widely held.

A modern scout must know a great many things – so many that it is almost impossible to detail them all, and for this reason a scout's work changes with the conditions under which he is working.

But I do not think that for a long time sufficient use was made of modern science in the equipment of the scout. A scout may, in a single two hours of his life, be a sniper, an observer, and the old-fashioned scout who has to go out to find out things at close range. He has to be essentially an individualist capable of seeing and seizing his opportunity. He must be a man of instant decision, who understands the value of cover and background, who possesses that quality which is very often born in men, a sense of direction.

His training was exceedingly difficult, and unless he had a natural aptitude, no amount of teaching was of any real practical value. Think what a difference it makes to a Commanding Officer to have in his battalion a certain number of men, however few, whom he can send out to obtain information, and who are so accurate and so dependable that he can always act upon their reports. There are hundreds of such men in the Lovat Scouts, but then, of course, the whole trend of their lives is towards observation, skilled movement, and accuracy. The man who has spent twenty years on the hill and who has counted the points on a thousand stags, who knows the difference between every track that he sets in a corrie, and who is never far from his telescope, is, when he goes to war, simply carrying into another sphere the normal activities of his life.

And yet there should be no difficulty in training a number of scouts in every battalion, *but the ideal scout, or rather the ideal scout section, in a regiment, should be looked up to. Their immense value should be realized, and due credit and honour given to them for their skill. The scouts of a battalion should be the pick of that battalion, and the fact that a man has attained the rank of scout should be signalized by his receiving extra pay and extra consideration.*

As long as war lasts it will be necessary to find out what is in the enemy's mind, and this is so important, that those who prove themselves capable of discovering and of giving warning of what is about to occur, should be objects of admiration and respect to all their comrades.

Of course there is another point, which struck one most strongly, and this was the examination of prisoners.

It may well be that a man cannot help being taken, whether through wounds or otherwise, but it is of the first importance that he should give away nothing to the enemy. For this reason, as scouts and anyone who has anything to do with any kind of Intelligence work are always put through a much more rigorous examination if they should be captured, we were very strongly against badges for scouts.

Let us take the ordinary Tommy. If he is captured, unless it unfortunately happens that he knows of some imminent move that is to be made, there is very little danger of his giving away anything, for the simple reason that he knows so little. But a scout is another matter. He knows all the posts in our line; he knows something of the system by which the various offshoots of Intelligence work are being operated. As he has been trained to observation of detail and deduction, he is a man who, if he can be got to speak, will reveal things of great value to the enemy.

The only two questions that a prisoner need answer are his name and regiment, but many and sinister are the tricks by which he may be beguiled.

A British officer who is supposed to have special knowledge is, let us imagine, captured by the Germans. He is wounded, and is taken up to the Headquarters of a German Division. He is examined, and, of course, gives away nothing. Now what happens? Very possibly a German officer comes to him and says: "Herr Captain, we deeply regret that there is no room for you in the officers' quarters in the Hospital. We trust that you will not object if you are put in a room with a British NCO." The officer, of course, says he does not object, and he goes into the room. There he will find a British NCO heavily bandaged and lying groaning upon his bed. It is inevitable, if they are two or three days together, that conversation will take place between them. The so-called British NCO is, however, simply a decoy. He is not wounded at all, and his business is, by clever questions, to extract certain information, which the British officer is supposed to possess.

Again, when men were taken prisoners, very often into the guardroom in which they were confined would be thrown another Britisher, bleeding and wounded, who would raise a tremendous outcry and declaim upon his wrongs. The newcomer, as a matter of fact, often was only a clever actor coached to his part, who was simply put into the guardhouse to ferret out information.

These are not isolated incidents, but a commonly accepted policy in the German Army. After all, it is natural enough, for a little bit of information may win a battle, and it was certainly held among our foes that the end justified the means.

But as the war went on, and these things came to knowledge, it needed some very clever work on the part of the Germans to obtain information from those who had been warned. Of course, as long as the world continues there are, one supposes, men who will undertake work of this kind, whether for money or urged on by some other motive. The motive may be good even. The decoy may be actuated by a really high form of patriotism. But not often. For the most part he is one of those men who have a touch of the traitor in them and who are in some way perverted in their minds.

Of course to be a decoy back at Divisional Headquarters is a safe and probably a paying job, but it is one, which must always leave a very nasty taste in the mouth.

So much for German methods of interrogation.

When we took German prisoners, they were very often in a state of pitiable fright, for they had been absolutely fed by their officers with stories of the most circumstantial nature of the habitual brutality of the British to their prisoners; and yet it was a fine sight to see a German prisoner, obviously afraid to his very bones, and yet absolutely determined to give away nothing. One really laboured under an almost incontrollable impulse to go and shake such a man by the hand. After all, courage of the lonely sort is surely the most glorious thing that we can hope to witness, and whether it is displayed upon our side or upon the other, one feels the better for having witnessed it.

Appendix A

The following is a programme, which has given excellent results when training Brigade, Divisional, Corps Observers and Lovat Scouts Observers.

1st Day	Lecture	Maps sand Conventional Signs
	Practical	Comparison of Map with the Ground
		Setting Maps
		Location of Points by Drawing Rays
2nd Day	Lecture	The Stalking Telescope
	Practical	Front Line Observation with Reports
		Instruction and Practice in Reading
		Map Co-ordinates
		Judging Distance
3rd Day	Lecture	Contours, Gradients, Slopes, etc
	Practical	Pegging Out Contours on the Ground
		Long Distance Observation with Reports
		Judging Distance
4th Day	Lecture	The Prismatic Compass
	Practical	Taking Bearings
		Working Out Mutual Visibility Problems
		Concave and Convex Slopes
		Drawing Slopes
5th Day	Lecture	The Use of the Protractor
	Practical	Plotting Bearings
		Re-section Problems
		Long distance Observation with Reports
6th Day	Lecture	Scales
	Practical	Road Traverse
		Filling in Conventional Signs and Contours
		Long Distance Observation with Reports
7th Day	Lecture	Use of Scouts and Observers in Attack and Defence
	Practical	Marching to Map Co-ordinates
		Selection of Positions for Observation Posts
		Front Line Observation with Reports
8th Day	Scheme	Bringing in the Use of Observers in Open Warfare
		Construction and Concealment of Observation Posts
		Taking Bearings with Compass
9th Day	Lecture	Front Line Observation
	Practical	Locating of Points by Drawing Rays
		Compass March (by Day)
10th Day	Lecture	Aeroplane Photographs
	Practical	Comparison of Photos with the Ground
		Re-section Problems

11th Day	Practical	Handing over and Relief of Observation Posts
		Using Telescope as Director
		Long Distance Observation with Reports
		Use of Director Board
12th Day	Practical	Making and Plotting a Road Traverse
		Making a Road Report
		Compass March (by Night)
13th Day	Practical	Enlarging Map and Constructing Scales
		Work with Director Board
14th Day		Recapitulation and Examinations

Appendix B

General Course at First Army SOS School

(From this the Battalion I. O. can frame Programmes of work to suit any period of Rest.)

The following lectures are given during the Course and are attended by all students except in the case of No 11, which is attended by the officers only.

1. Care of Arms and Grouping.
2. The Enfield 1914 pattern Rifle.
3. The Stalking Telescope.
4. General Lecture on Map-reading.
5. Patrolling and Scouting.
6. Elevations and Wind.
7. The Construction of Sniping and Forward OP's.
8. General Lecture on Telescopic-Sighted Rifles.
9. Duties of Scouts, Observers and Snipers in Attack and Defence.
10. Front Line Observation and Reports.
11. Duties of the Bn. Intelligence Officer.
12. Aeroplane photos, with Lantern Slides.
13. General Musketry Lecture.
14. Bayonet Training (by Supt P and BT First Army).
(Note: — Nos 13 and 14 are given on two evenings during the last week of the Course.)

In addition to the above and to the Programme, the officers go thoroughly into such subjects as:
1. Map-reading and Field Sketching.
2. Use of Prismatic Compass.
3. Enlarging Maps and Interpolation of Contours.
4. Panorama Sketching.
5. Adjustments and Care of Telescopic Sights.
6. Methods and Principles of Instruction.
7. Organization and Training.
8. Practical Study of Ground.

Practical work is also given to all students in the following subjects at night:
1. Patrolling.
2. Marching on Compass Bearings.
3. Concentration Marches with and without Box Respirators.
4. Siting and Construction of Posts.
5. Night Firing, and the Use of Field Glasses and Stalking Telescopes on Suitable Nights.

It will be seen that the two Sundays have been omitted; on these days the Range is open to all ranks for voluntary shooting under a qualified Instructor.

Instruction in the use of Armour Piercing; SAA, Disguising, Methods of Instruction, Practice in Map-reading, Taking Bearings, etc, etc, goes on continually while students await their turn to fire.

1st Morning	General talk on the objects of the Course and discipline during. Thorough examination of open sighted rifles for defects, Demonstration of Grouping and Holding. Grouping at 100 yards, followed by analysis of faults and correction of rifles where necessary.
Afternoon	Lecture: Care of Arms and Grouping. (Practical) Observation on a German Trench with Reports. Criticism of Reports.
2nd Morning	Lecture: The Stalking Telescope. (Practical) Repetition of failures in Grouping practice. Application at 2–300 yards. Observation of single shot strike.
Afternoon	Practical Observation. (a) On German Trench. (b) Open Country.
3rd Morning	Lecture: The Enfield 1914 pattern Rifle. (Practical) Judging Distance up to 600 yards. Snapshooting at 1–200 yards, 4 seconds' exposure. Application at 200 yards. Hawkins Position.
Afternoon	Practical Map-reading on the ground and long distance observations with Reports.
4th Morning	Lecture: General lecture on Map-reading. (Practical) Application at 4–500 yards. Application at unknown range (within 400 yards).
Afternoon	Demonstration: Use of Ground and Cover. (Practical) Practice in selecting, attaining and constructing hasty observation posts for open warfare. Cover from view rather than Cover from fire to be specialized in.
5th Morning	Lecture: Patrolling and Scouting. (Practical) Application at 300 yards. Snapshooting at 100 and 200 yards. 3 seconds' exposure.
Afternoon	Demonstration of Camouflage and its uses. (Practical) Scheme: Snipers are given an area of ground in which they must establish posts utilizing the material found on the spot for disguise. Observers select posts from which they can command the above area. The snipers will fire blanks from the posts they have selected at any observers who expose themselves and also endeavour to give the map reference of their targets. The observers endeavour to locate and give map references of the snipers' posts.

6th Morning	Lecture: Elevations and Wind. Demonstration: Building in battens for and spotting enemy snipers; actual practice in above; each student to locate at least two snipers. (Practical) Snapshooting combined with movement; students endeavour to advance unseen from 500 to 100 yards. Targets representing enemy heads appear at odd places and intervals in the butts.
Afternoon	Demonstration: Building in and use of Night Firing Boxes. Actual practice in above. Observation on a German trench, the appearance of which is altered by moving sandbags, loopholes, etc, with reports.
8th Morning	Lecture: The construction of Forward and Sniping OP's. (Practical) Patrolling with the use of Night Firing Goggles. Practice in the correct use of cover and in keeping touch. Application practice at unknown range.
Afternoon	Practice in marching by day on Compass bearings with and without Box-respirators.
9th Morning	Lecture: General lecture on telescopic sighted rifles. (Practical) Zeroing of telescopic sighted rifles.
Afternoon	Complete the zeroing of rifles. Long distance observation.
10th Morning	Lecture: Duties of scouts, observers and snipers in attack and defence. (Practical) Grouping at 100 yards with Telescopic sighted rifles. Practice in scouting in Open Country, with reports.
Afternoon	Scheme: Making "Good" woods and enclosed country with scouts and snipers.
11th Morning	Lecture: Front line observation and reports. (Practical) Application at 200 yards with telescopic sighted rifles. Snapshooting at 1–200 yards, 3 seconds' exposure.
Afternoon	Concentration march. Students are put into four parties, each representing a platoon. They are given a map co-ordinate at which they must concentrate at a given time. Signals representing Gas Alarm are given, when all students put on their box-respirators and continue the march.
12th Morning	Lecture: Duties of the Bn Intelligence Officer. (Practical) Application at 3–400 yards. Observation on a German trench.
Afternoon	Scheme: To demonstrate the use of Scouts and Snipers as a protective advanced screen to infantry in open or semi-open warfare.
13th Morning	Lecture: Aeroplane Photos, with Lantern Slides. Practical study of aeroplane photographs on the actual ground depicted in the photo.

Afternoon   Examinations in Long distance and Front line observations.

15th and 16th.   Oral examinations. Mutual Instruction. Written examination. Examination of notebooks. Competition shoots.

Note:— The above programme is only given as a guide; changes in sequence must often occur through inclemency of the weather.

Appendix C

The following are the rough notes used for some of the Lectures given at the First Army School of SOS in France.

Part I

Care of Arms, Grouping and Range Practices

It is essential that the Sniper shall have a really clean rifle if he is to obtain the extreme accuracy that is required of him. By a clean rifle I mean a rifle in the cleaning of which not only have all the normal precautions been taken, but, in addition, the bore has received a very high polish. This high polish is of great importance to accurate shooting, and to be efficient as a Sniper you must be far more accurate than the average Service Shot. Hence the necessity for going rather deeply into Care of Arms.

Avoidable Causes of Inaccuracy

Oily barrel

Is a great cause of inaccuracy, as the resistance offered to the bullet in its passage down the bore is varied, and thus the shooting of the rifle becomes inconsistent.

Oily Breech

This prevents correct "seizing" in the breech, and tends to lead to a blowback. If a blowback occurs there is a loss of driving power, muzzle velocity is decreased and accuracy is lost.

Cordwear

Is caused by misuse of the pull-through, and usually occurs at the muzzle, but in cases of extreme negligence it may be found in the chamber. When it occurs at the muzzle, gases escape through the cord groove as the bullet is leaving, thus forcing it in the opposite direction. If in the chamber, it is a source of weakness, and a burst chamber may be the result.

Fixing the Bayonet

Musketry Regulations inform us that with the "SMLE" the effect of fixing the bayonet is to throw your shot 18 inches high at 200 yards' range. This is because the extra weight slows down the vibration, and thus converts a *negative* into a *positive* jump. Hence, as a Sniper, you will fire without your bayonet fixed.

(Note:— From tests carried out at this First Army School of SOS it would appear that Musketry regulations greatly over-estimate the effect caused by fixing the bayonet.)

Hold

Unless the Sniper reproduces the same hold for each shot and when he rests his rifle rests it always at the same point (for preference the middle band), his shooting can never be consistent.

Ammunition

Different makes of SAA give slightly different elevations on the target. This is because the Powders burn at different rates, thus slightly altering the jump.

Warped Woodwork

The fore-end is fitted so as not to influence the barrel when firing. The barrel must be able to lie perfectly straight as each shot leaves it. If the fore-end is warped (and warped fore-ends are common), the barrel will be unable to lie as was intended, and erratic shooting will result.

Causes

1. Wet entering between the barrel and the fore-end.
2. Unequal dryness such as caused by rifle lying in hot sun or in front of fire.
3. Dry woodwork.
4. Twisting of wood through insufficient seasoning before use.

Prevention of

Oil all woodwork daily, ensuring that the oil penetrates between the hand-guard, fore-end and barrel.

Cure of

Armourer refits fore-end.

Some unavoidable causes

Nickelling or metallic fouling

Is really, an obstruction in the bore caused by a portion of the envelope of the bullet becoming brazed on the surface of the bore. It is a cause of great inaccuracy, and its presence should always be looked for. When found, it must be removed. This should be done by an Armourer.

Erosion

Is the gradual increase in the size of the bore and is caused through the heat generated by the gases slightly fusing the metal. The gases rushing over the metal carry away minute particles of the steel. This is the factor, which decides "The Life of the Barrel." for purposes of real accuracy.

Drift

Is the continual deviation of the bullet in the direction of the rifling. About one minute, ie, one inch per 100 yards, must be allowed for this at the longer ranges in sniping.

Other Definitions

Superficial Fouling

The fouling that appears in the bore immediately after firing. It is then quite soft and easily removed, but if allowed to remain, it becomes hard, difficult to remove and, by attracting moisture from the air, begins the rusting process.

Internal Fouling

Fouling that actually gets below the surface of the metal when firing; this gradually sweats its way to the surface and should be removed as it appears.

(Note:— If cleaned with really boiling water, the pores are reopened, internal fouling is removed, and thus the cause of sweating is done away with. The Barrel must, however, be dried immediately, or the cure will be worse than the complaint.)

Corrosion

Is the black pockmark or indentation left in the bore after removing rust.

Cleaning Rods

Finally it is suggested that a cleaning-rod properly used is better than a pull-through: each Battalion is authorized to hold 32 of these Rods on Charge. (See GRO's 512, 540 and 2,094.)

Grouping and Range Practices

It must be understood that Grouping with the Open Sights is a definite test of (a) the rifle, and (b) the man.

Grouping is a practical system of locating faults, and it is of the utmost importance that such faults, having once been located, should at once be corrected. It should also be clearly understood that a man's average group at a given range, ie, 100 yards, will (except for the error of the day) be the measure of his capacity at all ranges. For instance, if his average at 100 yards be a three inch group, his best standard will be a six inch group at 200 yards, nine inch group at 300 yards, 12 inch group at 400 yards, and so on.

Unless this fact is clearly understood, we shall have our men making shot corrections when actually shooting up to standard, and if this is done, consistent shooting can never be obtained.

Lessons to be Learnt from a Group

1. If a man makes a vertical group, it is fairly safe to assume that he is making one of the following errors:
    (a) Varying amount of foresight taken.
    (b) Varying point of Aim.
    (c) Not restraining his breathing when trigger-pressing.

2. If he makes a lateral group, his error will be usually found among the following:
    (a) Incorrect centering of foresight.
    (b) Varying point of Aim.
    (c) Bad let-off.

3. If he gets a good group, but wide of the aiming mark, it will be safe to assume that his rifle is throwing wide and should be corrected at once by alteration of fore-sight. For this reason the Armourer or other qualified person should be present when grouping is being carried out.

4. If a man's shots are widely scattered, it will be necessary to carry out the Analysis of faults, i.e.:

    R. Test Rifle.
    A. Test Aim.
    T. Test Trigger-pressing.
    S. Test Sight.

You should by this time have discovered the fault, but remember it is of no use having found it unless you can cure it before proceeding further.

5. If the rifle were correct, the point of Mean impact should be five inches above the point of Aim. If incorrect, the foresight should be altered. The following can be got on indent for this purpose.

    Cramp RSLME
    Supply of foresights in nine different heights.

Range Practices

Nothing definite can be laid down on account of the lack of uniform targets, ranges, etc, but the following hints may be of value:

1. If a liaison be cultivated between Battalion Sniping officers in the Brigade, it will be easy to improvise a Range and Target for the use of the Battalion in rest.

2. When in divisional rest, it is usually possible to find a Range ready for use in the Training Area.

3. Excellent work and all Zeroing can be done on even a 30-yard range by the really keen officer.

4. Training in shooting should be carried out with an Open and *not a Telescopic* sighted rifle, which should be kept for

    (a) Snapping Practice.
    (b) Shooting in order to Zero.
    (c) Killing the enemy.

It is important that the barrels of these rifles should not be worn out in practice shooting.

5. All training should be made progressive and where possible competitive.

6. The first essential is extreme accuracy, after which the instructor must coach up for rapid snapshooting, the ultimate standard being looked upon as the ability to get off a really good shot under two seconds.

7. Always start with a Grouping Practice and eliminate faults as they are discovered.

8. Re-zero Telescopic sighted rifles to ascertain that they have maintained their correctness each time you are out of the trenches, and arm only your best shots with these rifles.

9. Improvise cover on the Range and make all Snipers' fire practices under as near as possible Service Conditions.

10. Although normally he will not fire Rapid, keep your sniper efficient in this valuable art.

11. You may at any time become a casualty, therefore train your NCOs to carry on in your absence.

Part II

Patrolling and Scouting

Patrols and Patrolling

The importance of patrolling cannot be exaggerated. It is a means of keeping in touch with the enemy and of obtaining much valuable information.

In open warfare, we must patrol day and night. In trench warfare, observation to a great extent does away with patrolling by day. We should always look upon the ground between the hostile armies as being ours and should *make* it so by patrols. This gives our men a greater sense of security and also has the effect of destroying the enemy *morale.*

Patrolling is looked upon by some as being particularly dangerous work. This is not so if patrols are carefully carried out by trained men.

Training beforehand is essential; to send out untrained men in a haphazard manner is worse than useless.

No patrol should go out except for a distinct and definite object.

Types of Patrols in Trench Warfare

Reconnaissance Patrols

Are the work of scouts who go out on some specific mission. Numbers should be as small as possible. A party of two or three will probably obtain the best results.

Fighting Patrols

Should consist of Lewis gun and gunners, bombers and scouts. Strength 10–15. Object to disperse enemy working parties, to engage enemy patrols, to obtain identifications.

Note:— It may often be necessary to combine these patrols; the Fighting Patrol going out to form a screen in rear, while the Reconnaissance Patrol pushes forward to complete its task. This has the effect of giving the Reconnaissance Patrol confidence, of assisting them to pass back any casualties they may suffer, and, in fact, provides them with an Advanced Headquarters from which they carry out their reconnaissance. The system is particularly useful, and, in fact, necessary, where a great distance separates the opposing lines.

Protective Patrols

Should consist mainly of bombers, and are used in front of our wire, or between isolated posts. Numbers depend on circumstances. Object: Protection of our line from surprise attacks.

Open Warfare

It is not necessary here to classify definitely. The Reconnoitring Patrol should always be prepared to fight. In fact, all Patrols, at all times, should be *fully organized self-contained fighting units.* Numbers depend on conditions, but Scouts will be largely used.

126

Training

The general principles of training both for Trench and Open Warfare are a thorough training in the following:
1. Map Reading.
2. Compass Work.
3. Reports.
4. Use of Ground and Cover.
5. Reconnoitring through Periscopes and by means of Aeroplane Photographs and Maps by day, the ground over which patrol must pass at night, and selecting, the best method of approach.
6. Actual Patrolling by day and night.
7. Keeping touch.

Formations

Nothing definite can be laid down, as, of necessity, formations will vary with the prevailing conditions. It is essential, however, that all formations shall be so simple as to ensure that they can be maintained even on the darkest night and when working over very rough ground.

The Lewis gun, when it forms a part of a Patrol, must be well protected and in such a position as will enable it to be used at a moment's notice.

The Officer or NCO in charge should always lead the Patrol, and there should be a Second-in-Command, whose position should be in the centre and rear of the Patrol; he will specialize in keeping the men in their proper places and maintaining touch.

Equipment

The rifle often hampers movement, particularly when crawling, but it is essential that both this and fighting order be carried when patrolling in open warfare. In trench warfare it should usually be sufficient to carry the rifle, a bandolier of SAA, the web belt with bayonet and scabbard attached, a bomb in the pocket and a compass. Steel helmets should not be taken, the cap-comforter being worn instead.

If necessary to fix the bayonet, such as when rushing an isolated post, it should be fixed with the scabbard still on; both bayonet and scabbard should be well oiled; the scabbard can then be taken off quietly just prior to the rush.

Instructions to be Given

Before going out personnel should be given:
1. All known information.
2. An opportunity to examine by day through periscope, by aeroplane photographs and maps, the ground to be covered at night.
3. The object of the patrol.
4. The password.

Everything that is liable to give information or identification, if captured, must be carefully collected before the party goes out.

All men in the Garrison and battalions on right and left must know when the patrol is out, and also the password.

The patrol leader, both on leaving and returning, will himself pass the word along to this effect. This is very important. He cannot forecast how long he will be away, or the point at which he will return; therefore, the trench garrison must be prepared to receive him at any time or place.

General

Patrols often give themselves away by leaving their own trench in a careless manner. The firing of rifles and lights, should continue as usual when a patrol is out, but in such a manner as not to interfere with the patrol. Two patrols should never be sent out on the same front at the same time, as this only leads to their mistaking each other for the enemy. Often, the most suitable time for patrolling is when the weather conditions are very bad. In addition to taking precautions against Verey lights, men on patrol can often take advantage of their brightness to obtain the information required.

A Form of Patrol Report

Patrol Report
Blankshire Regiment.
Night of 12–13th/6/17
Ref Map Sheet 54 S.E.I.

Composition	Time and Point of Exit	Object	Information gained and action taken	Time and Point of Return
1 Offr. and 1 o/Rk. Lt Tew Pte Dew	11pm Trench Willow Walk A6a92.85	To report on enemy wire from High Command Redoubt to No Man's Cottage	Gap in wire at Points No. 1 A5a65.75 2 A5b20.35 3 A5d85.87 Width in Gaps: 1 about 4 yards. 2 ” 2 ” 3 ” 3 ” Average depth of wire 10–15 yds. General condition: High, barbed, and fairly strong.	2am Trench Willow Walk A6a95.87

Handed in at 3am.
Date: 13/6/17.

(Sgd.) R G A Tew, Lieutenant, Blankshire Regiment.

Note:— These headings, etc., are given as a guide. They will vary according to the nature of the information required, and the circumstances under which the Patrol is working.

Part III

The Stalking Telescope

Apart from the regular issue of G S Telescopes, there are now in the BEF about 40,000 or 50,000 more or less high-class telescopes. These have been obtained from all kinds of sources, from deerstalkers, yachtsmen, etc, and the care and use of these glasses has become a matter of great importance.

Care and Cleaning

The first thing to remember is that the lenses of all telescopes are made of very soft glass, and that this glass is polished to a very high degree. A few scratches on the outer surface of the object glass will negate the value of the best telescope. When the telescope is first taken from its case, a light film of dust will usually be found to have formed on the object glass. This should be flicked off with a handkerchief, and if any polishing is necessary, it should be done with a piece of chamois leather or well-washed piece of four-by-two; this cleaning material should be free from grit, and should be carried in a pocket or in the pay-book, where it will be kept clean. Over 50 per cent of the telescopes in use, in or about the front line, have been scratched more or less badly, owing to the neglect of this simple precaution.

Special attention should be paid to the cleaning of the objective lens, which is liable to become covered with dust owing to its position in the telescope and the opening and closing of the draws.

Never on any account touch the glass with the finger or thumb. If the glass be allowed to get damp, fogging will result. To cause the fogging to evaporate, remove object glass and eyepiece, lay the telescope out in the sun or in a warm room. Never permit the metal work to get hotter than the temperature of your hand, otherwise the Canada Balsam (which is used to join the concave and convex lenses in the object-glass of all high telescopes, except the GS) will melt. If the draws get wet, they must be thoroughly dried and slightly lubricated. The same applies to the sunshade. When an officer is inspecting telescopes, he should inspect the cases also. In screwing tubes or cells into place, great care must be taken not to damage the threads. It is often as well to turn the screw the wrong way with a gentle pressure; the threads will then come into correct engagement, and a slight click may be heard.

The General Service Telescope

As has been stated above, Canada Balsam is not used between the lenses of the object glass of the G S telescope. When a G S Telescope has been taken to pieces, the only difficulty experienced in assembling it again will be in the replacing of the lenses forming the object glass. To do this two rules must be remembered:
1. The convex lens is always the nearest to the object, and, therefore, must be replaced first.
2. On the side of the lenses forming the object glass an arrowhead will be found cut into the glass.

Before the lenses are put back the arrowhead must be completed, and the middle of the arrow must be allowed to slide over the barb or raised line in the cell.

Rules for Use

1. Always extend your sunshade (more OP's have been given away by the light shining upon the object-glass of telescopes than in any other way.)
2. Always mark your focus by scratching a circular ring on the focusing draw. (This will allow you to focus your glass correctly and quickly before putting it to your eye.)
3. Always pull out or push in the draws of your telescope with a clock-wise circular motion and keep them slightly lubricated.
4. Always carry your telescope slung on your body. If you take it off and let it travel in a lorry or car, the jolting will almost certainly ruin it.
5. Always use a rest when observing.
6. When looking into the sun, make a sunshade nine inches or a foot long to fit on the short sun-shade of the telescope. This will give you great assistance when the sun is over the German lines. It is a trick borrowed from the chamois hunters of the Pyrenees.
7. Remember that when there is a mirage, you will get better results with a low than with a high power of magnification. Conditions in France are more suitable to a magnification of under than over twenty-five. Excellent work can be done in the front line with a glass that magnifies only ten times. If the high-power eyepiece is used for any special purpose when reconnaissance is finished, it should be replaced by a low-power eye-piece.
8. When searching a given sector of ground or trench divide it into "fields of view" work slowly allowing each field to overlap. Never leave any suspicious-looking object without having ascertained what it is and why it is there.
9. Slight movement is more easily detected if you do not look straight at the object. Always look a little left, right, high or low. Keenest vision is at the edges of the eye. This particularly applies to dusk or dawn.
10. When your object is found, consider:
    (a) Distance.
    (b) Shape.
    (c) Colour.
    (d) Size.
    (e) Position.
Use each detail to check other details; for instance, if you can distinguish the state cockade upon a German cap, you may be certain that you are not more than two hundred yards distant.
11. Do not forget that good results can be obtained on clear starlight or moonlight nights by the use of night-glasses or telescopes, especially if working in conjunction with a Lewis or Vickers Gun. Generally speaking, the bigger the object-glass and the lower the magnification, the better will be the results obtainable at night.
12. In trench warfare a really good glass-man working from our front line by day can make a most valuable wire reconnaissance.
13. Remember that the conditions of visibility are constantly changing; an object which is indistinct at eleven o'clock may become quite clear at eleven-five.

14. Always be ready to avail yourself of natural conditions. The visibility after a rain shower is almost always good; it shows up wire and gaps in the wire, paths, ground traversed by patrols, etc. The best season for "spotting" OP's is autumn, when the leaves fall and the grass withers.

15. It is a good thing to disguise the whole of the telescope by use of sandbags or other material around it. Great care must be taken to ascertain that such disguise is kept free from dust or grit.

Part IV

Front Line Observation and Reports

Remember that straws show which way the wind blows and that apparently trivial information maybe of great importance if considered in correct perspective. For instance, three small parties of Germans seen in front of a battalion sector is not an item of much interest, but if such parties are seen by all or most of the observers on a divisional front, enemy movement of importance is indicated so include everything observed which is of the slightest importance.

Remember that your report passes through the hands of the Battalion Intelligence Officer, and by him the information it contains is passed on to Brigade, thence to Division, and so on. During the whole of this process, the information is weighed, sifted, and compared over and over again. Hence, that which really proves to be of no importance will be eliminated, while that which is of value will reach those to whom it may be of use.

Remember that you are in close touch with the enemy, and that you, and you only, are responsible for the observation of his forward area. You must not rely upon the Divisional or Corps Observers to do this work for you.

When taking over a post for the first time, you must study the ground carefully and get to know the exact location of all prominent objects. Then, in a few days' time, you will be capable of giving map locations of targets without bearings.

It is of little or no use to look for movement until you know your front by heart. The GOOD observer is the man who can almost see the co-ordinates lying on the ground. In this way some of the Lovat Scouts can give the map references of a moving object as it moves, without a glance at the map.

The best times of the day for you, as a front-line observer, are dawn and dusk. Ration parties, working parties, reliefs, etc, are all waiting to move forward at dusk, and much good work can be done by picking up these targets and reporting them to the Artillery. The same or similar parties can often be seen returning at dawn, particularly after a night during which our harassing fire has been heavy.

Again, a misty day – although the definition obtained through your telescope is not so clear as usual – is often excellent for observation of the enemy's frontline system. On such days, through a false sense of security, the enemy often shows himself in concealed posts, etc, which he would never give away by carelessness during clearer weather.

Always note time (signal time) and map co-ordinates of anything observed.

If anything of importance be seen, such as abnormal movement, suspected reliefs, etc, report them at once. Don't wait until you come off duty.

All targets should be reported as soon as possible to the Artillery.

If there are any Artillery OP's in your vicinity, they should be visited, as the occupants can often assist you by "placing" objects, the exact location of which you yourself are doubtful about. The Artillery Observers should be shown all tracks where movement has been observed to enable them to get a gun trained on to them.

All new enemy work must be followed closely and its object, if possible, ascertained.

Take a pride in extreme accuracy, let a direct statement represent fact, but do not hesitate to include information of which you are not quite certain. You must, however, never fail to indicate clearly the degree of accuracy or certainty, which you yourself feel. Useful words for qualifying your statements are as follows:

Possibly;

About;

Probably;

Approximately, etc, etc.

Remember that your duty is rather to observe and report your observations than to interpret what you see. At the same time, give personal impressions. These may start a new line of thought in the minds of those who read your reports; also, if two or three observers, from different points, think that they have seen a certain thing, then there is at least a strong probability that a foundation existed for their belief.

Realize that your observation is part of a huge net which is continually trawling the whole enemy world for information, and see to it that not even the smallest fry slip through the meshes for which you are personally responsible.

For purposes of actual observation, a rough logbook must be kept in the sniping or observation post. In this book everything seen should be noted as it occurs. From it each evening the information must be set out under suitable headings and your report rendered to the Battalion Intelligence Officer. Customs vary in battalions, but the following list of headings may help you in this matter

Operations, Enemy

1. Artillery
2 Trench Mortars (TM's) No. and Calibre, of projectiles and targets
3. Grenades
4. A.A. Guns … Activity.
5. MG Fire – Methods and Targets.
6. Rifle Fire – Methods and Targets.

Movement, Enemy

1. Aircraft.
2. Trains.
3. Transport.
4. Men actually seen.
5. Indication of movement (periscopes, loopholes, etc).
6. Patrols. (Seen, heard or encountered.)
(Note:— Time and place must always be given.)

Battalion Intelligence Report to Brigade

The subject matter forming this falls naturally under the following main headings:
1. Operations. (Enemy.)
2. Movement. (Enemy.)
3. Work. (Enemy.)

4. Signals. (Enemy.)
5. General Intelligence.
6. Weather.

Under these six main headings are the following sub-headings:

Work, Enemy

(a) Changes visible in enemy line.
(b) Working parties seen or heard.
(c) New wire observed or reported by patrols.

Signals, Enemy:

(a) Flash lamps.
(b) Verey lights. Full description of and any apparent results.
(c) Rockets.

General Intelligence

Information of a doubtful or uncertain nature, general impressions, etc.

Weather

(a) General conditions.
(b) Light and visibility during the day. .
(c) Wind, its strength and direction.

In some Brigades, reports on our own operations, particularly observation of our own Artillery and TM fire, are required in the Battalion Intelligence Reports, but this is a mistaken policy.

A Form of Observation Report

Observation Report

No. of Post (Map Ref.): Teapot Post N33c55.90
Sheet 17A N.E.
Time on Duty: 7am to 10am
Date: 20.6.18.
Observers on Duty, Name, Rank and Regt.
      H. Smith   Pte
      G. Shaw   L/Cpl
Wind: Gentle SW
Visibility: Fair.

Time.	*Map Ref.*	*Event.*	*Remarks.*	
7.30 a.m.	M39d45.35	1 German N.C.O. and 14 Ptes.	Ptes. carrying wood, corrugated iron and sandbags. Wearing caps with red bands. Badges not visible.	Probably working on entrance to dug-out at M39c78.65
8.45 a.m.	Over trench at Mz8c36.03	Enemy Aeroplane Pilot and 1 other	Opened fire on trench. Flying low, about 700 feet. Flew off in S.W. direction. Not fired on by our men.	Enemy probably expects concentration in this area.
(Changed over 9 a.m.)			Observer—Shaw. Writer—Smith.	
9.15 a.m.	G30a40.92	Horse transport	15 wagons, 4 horse, all very heavily loaded, moving N. on Vitry-Douai Road.	Possibly ammunition or heavy material. Had difficulty in ascending slight hill.

Relieved at 10am. Observer: Shaw
Handed in at 10.15am. Writer: Smith.
(Signed)   H. SMITH.
            G. SHAW.

Part V

Some Uses of Scouts, Observers and Snipers in Attack, Defence and Open Warfare

It is difficult to lay down any hard and fast rules on this subject, as so much depends upon the prevailing conditions. The following notes should therefore be looked upon as tentative hints or suggestions.

To commence, it is well to remember that these men, in addition to being fully-trained soldiers, have received specialist training in such subjects as map reading, obtaining and reporting information, scouting, accurate shooting, etc; therefore their value to the Company Commander, whether in Attack or Defence, in trench warfare or in open warfare, has been enhanced, and he should keep this in mind when making his dispositions.

Prior to attack on any given objective, the Scouts and Observers can obtain much valuable information; in fact, the actual plans for local attack will often depend upon the information so obtained.

The following are some of the points that should be ascertained either by direct observation or patrolling or both:

1. Location of enemy MG's and strong points.
2. Whether the enemy is holding his line continuously or by isolated posts; if the latter, the location of each post should, if possible, be ascertained.
3. If our wire-cutting operations have been successful, and the location and width of the gaps.

Vigorous patrolling should take place for some time prior to attack, to ensure that the enemy is driven out of "No Man's Land," thus enabling us to "jump off" from a point as near as possible to the enemy line.

The Snipers can, by making each enemy periscope and loophole a target, render the enemy to a great extent blind in Front Line Observation. Before the actual assault has commenced, our snipers can be established in shell holes in "No Man's Land from which they can command any known machine-gun emplacements. They should always carry a few rounds of armour-piercing SAA, and should look upon the breech casing of the gun as their target rather than the gunners. (Your good sniper will appreciate the fact that one hit on the breech-casing of a machine-gun with armour-piercing SAA will definitely put the gun out of action, as it ruins the vital portion, *ie*, "the recoiling portion" of the gun.)

After the objective has been gained, the snipers should push forward beyond our new line and establish themselves in shell holes or in old trenches. From these positions their fire will be of great value in conjunction with the Lewis gunners in keeping down the enemy during consolidation.

The Scouts should be able to fill in the dispositions of the troops and maintain touch with flanking units; they should form part of exploiting patrols, locate the enemy's new positions and ascertain their attitude, *ie*, whether they are demoralized and retiring in disorder or whether they are under control and likely to counterattack.

The Observers must be in a position from which they can watch the whole of the attack and must be provided with a means of communication whereby they can constantly report upon the situation. After the objective has been gained, they can push forward and locate enemy machine-guns and battery positions; this will be comparatively easy as, if the enemy is putting up a fight, machine-guns, etc, will be advertising themselves.

The Brigade and Divisional Observers will also be in positions from which they can follow the whole of the attack and will constantly report its progress. They should particularly watch for any massing of enemy troops in the back areas for counter-attack.

In Defence

The Snipers can be of great value in defence, and should be given a definite "battle station." If the attack be delivered in daylight, the snipers' special task should be to pick off the leaders, and members of machine-gun and *minenwerfer* detachments. If the enemy succeed in occupying our trenches, the snipers must have in readiness alternative posts that command stretches of our trenches; they will thus be in a position to inflict heavy losses upon the new occupants. In this way and by working in conjunction with Bombers, they can do much to prevent the enemy from establishing himself.

The Observers can, in defence, find out much valuable information, and the good observer can usually foretell an enemy attack by carefully watching for the following signs of offensive operation:

1. Construction of new TM emplacements.
2. Registration of new TM's.
3. Increased artillery registration.
4. Bridging of trenches.
5. Cutting of wire.
6. Additional dressing stations instituted.
7. Signboards erected.
8. Unusual amount of movement in back areas.
9. Increased aerial activity.
10. Reconnaissance of front by enemy officers.

Open Warfare

In open and semi-open warfare it is essential that observers push forward from one post to another. They must keep in touch with the attack, with flanking units and with headquarters.

The most important duties of scouts and snipers will be reconnaissance. By pushing forward as an advanced screen to cover the advance, they can collect much valuable information and, if correctly organized, can get such information back quickly to the officers whom it concerns. The following are some of the things upon which they should report:

1. Where the enemy are and if holding a continuous line or isolated posts.
2. Condition of roads, etc.
3. Best approaches for Infantry, Machine-guns, Artillery, etc.
4. Any obstacles such as rivers, etc, and the best means of negotiating them.

5. Places, which are exposed to fire.

6. Any topographical features from which the enemy can be commanded.

In fact, there is no limit to the amount of useful information that scouts and snipers can obtain. They can also be of extreme value in working round and cutting off isolated posts. They may also form a thin but effective firing line that can delay considerably a small counter-attack and thus enable their unit to complete the, of necessity, hasty preparations for holding its gains.

Part VI

The Enfield 1914 Pattern "Snipers Rifle"

As each battalion now holds three of these rifles on charge for sniping purposes (GRO 3567), it is essential that your snipers shall understand the main differences between this and the RSMLE.

It is as well to understand at once that a far higher degree of accuracy can be obtained from the Enfield 1914 than from the RSMLE, and this is the reason why it has been issued to snipers. The higher degree of accuracy is due to two main causes:

1. The rifles so issued have been specially selected from thousands of other rifles of the same pattern, on account of their accuracy, after severe and exhaustive tests.

2. The rifle is fitted with an aperture or peep slight, which, as will be readily acknowledged by most expert riflemen, possesses a great advantage over the open U or V backsight. It is therefore unnecessary to focus the backsight, and the blur, which is unavoidable when aiming with the open U or V backsight is entirely absent with the aperture or peep sight.

The following are the main differences, which must be noted and thoroughly understood in order to get the best results from the new rifle.

The Sight

The rear of the body is made in the form of a bed in which the sight should always lie when not in use. In this position the aperture battle sight can be used if desired, but it should seldom be necessary for the sniper to use this sight. The battle sight is actually sighted to hit on the aiming mark at about 400 yards' range.

The sight leaf is hinged on to the sight bed and is raised to an angle of about 90° from the sight bed for use. There are in all four positions in which it will rest. (See diagram 1.)

1. At an angle of about 45° from the sight bed; this is the most convenient position for "sight setting."

2. At an angle of about 90°; this is the position when in use.

3. At an angle of about 135°.

4. At an angle of about 180°.

The two last positions have been made possible so as to avoid damaging the sight by accidentally knocking it, if raised against undergrowth, etc, when skirmishing.

Note:— The bolt lever must not be raised and drawn back when the sight is in No 4 position, as if this is done the battle sight is sheared off.

Elevation

The elevation is obtained by raising a slide on the leaf. This slide carries the aperture, and, when set, is held in position by a spring-catch adjustment on the right of the leaf. The leaf is graduated from 200 to 1100 yards in hundreds of yards, and from 1100 to 1650 yards in fifties. The reading line is situated in the centre of the slide, and care must be taken to point out this fact clearly, otherwise men are apt to take readings from the top or bottom of the slide.

Fine Adjustment

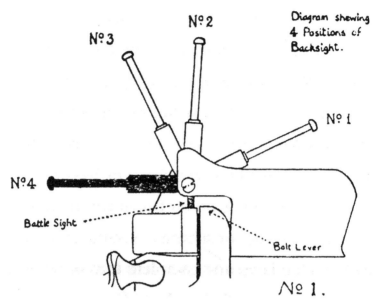

Diagram showing four positions of Backsight

The sight is fitted with a fine adjustment in the form of a worm screw with a milled head. By rotating the milled head clockwise we raise the elevation, and by turning it anti-clockwise we lower it. The top of the milled head is marked off into three divisions, each of which is equivalent to one minute of angle, which is about 1" per 100 yards of the range. Thus at 100 yards it would equal 1" rise, or fall, on the target; at 200 yards 2"; at 300 yards 3", and so on. A reading line is marked on the top of the sight leaf to enable these minute adjustments to be made. (See diagram.)

The advantage of a fine adjustment screw on this principle lies in the fact that, without alteration of foresight, the rifle can be zeroed with exactness in a vertical sense, for any individual hold. Thus: If a man, when zeroing his rifle at 100 yards' range, finds the point of mean impact to be three inches low, or high, he has only to remember that he must first reproduce on his backsight the range for which he is firing, and then add, or subtract, three minutes of elevation, ie, by giving the milled head one complete turn or revolution in the required direction; he will then have his correct zero for that particular range. (*Note*: Before starting to zero at 100 yards, he must raise the sight to 200 yards, and then takeoff three minutes; this is equivalent to setting his sight to 100 yards (which is not marked). With the sight so set, the "point of mean impact" should be 1½ inches to 2 inches above the point of aim.)

In addition, the fine adjustment can be used to overcome the difficulty of not having the sight calibrated to read to fifties at the closer ranges. By memorizing the following table, the sniper will have no difficulty in adjusting his sight to 250, 350, 450 yards, and so on:

To raise from	To	Add to column 1
200 yards	250 yards	1 minute
300 yards	350 yards	1 1/2 minutes
400 yards	450 yards	2 minutes
500 yards	550 yards	2 1/2 minutes
600 yards	650 yards	3 minutes

The table has not been taken further, as 600 yards is the limit of "individual effort."

Lateral Zero

If there should be a lateral error when zeroing, the foresight should be moved as in the RSMLE, except that the cramp is made to fit over and through the foresight protectors, and, as there is no nose-cap to remove, it is a simpler operation.

Aim, How Taken

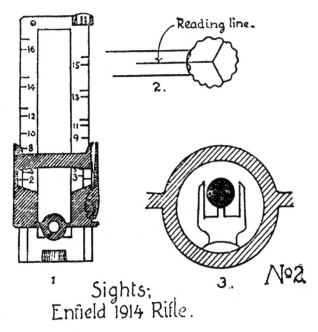

Sights: Enfield 1914 Rifle

Diagram 2 will illustrate far better than a word picture how aim should be taken. The main thing is to look *through* the aperture, and not *at it.* The foresight will be centred in the aperture, and the tip of it placed at 6 o'clock in the ordinary way. (*Note*: It will be found that with very little practice the eye will instinctively centre the foresight, and that aiming, with this sight, will in reality simply be the action of holding the tip of the foresight on to 6 o'clock.)

The Magazine

The magazine holds five rounds only and is constructed in such a manner as to permit the magazine platform to rise and engage the face of the bolt head when the magazine is empty. This advertises the fact that "reloading" is necessary. At the same time, it prevents giving practice in "rapid manipulation of the bolt," unless the "depressors magazine platform," or a coin such as a franc (which will serve the same purpose) be used to hold down the platform, thus enabling the bolt to pass freely through the bolt-way when the magazine is empty.

It is of simple construction, consisting of three parts only: the platform, the spring and the bottom plate. To remove: press the point of a bullet into the hole that will be found in the bottom plate, in front of the trigger guard, then push downwards and in the direction of the trigger; this releases the spring and allows the magazine to be removed and cleaned. To replace: reverse the above process. Care must be taken when loading to ensure that the charger is placed vertically in the charger guide; if allowed to lean forward, the first cartridge will foul the padding of the magazine, and loading will become difficult.

There is little possibility of a jam if the bolt way, the breech and the magazine are kept clean.

Safety Devices

1. The Safety Catch. — This is similar to the RSMLE, but is on the opposite side, ie, the right side of the body. If the thumb piece is turned over to the rear, it performs two actions. (*a*) Rotates the half-moon on the eccentric stem until it engages in the recess in the cocking piece, thus preventing the cocking piece from going forward if the trigger be accidentally pressed. (*b*) Pushes forward the locking bolt plunger until it is engaged in the locking bolt recess in the bolt lever, thus preventing the rotation of the bolt.

2. Bolt Lever. — This when turned down, *ie*, when the breech is closed, fits into a recess in the body of the rifle, and ensures that the bolt cannot he blown back, even should the resisting lugs give way.

3. The Safety Stud. — This is in direct communication with the sear, and is constructed in such a manner as to ensure that the sear cannot be depressed without the safety stud rising. On the under side of the bolt is a recess which comes immediately over the safety stud when the bolt lever is turned fully down. It is, therefore, impossible to press the trigger, which depresses the sear, until the bolt lever is fully turned down and the action sealed.

Gas Escapes

Of these there are three. On the right of the hood; on the under side of the bolt, one in front and the other in rear of the extractor ring. They perform the same duties as the gas escapes in the RSMLE, except that the one in front of the extractor ring prevents air pockets – which would act as brakes – from forming.

Pull Off

This is slightly different to that of the RSMLE, the first pull being from 2 to 3lbs, and the second from 5 to 6lbs. The first pull is comparatively long, and it is necessary to obtain, by practice, the correct "trigger squeeze" before firing the rifle for the first time.

Care and Cleaning

In order to take full advantage of the rifle, it is essential that it be kept absolutely clean; the following parts should receive special attention:

The Bore – This should always carry a high polish.

The Sights – Must be kept free from oil, and the aperture free from fluff.

The Hood – Must always be free from oil and dirt, as it contains the recesses in which the resisting lugs work, and if dirt be allowed to gather there, the shock of discharge cannot be evenly taken on both sides, and accurate shooting under these conditions is unattainable.

The Breech – Must be kept clean and free from oil by means of the stick, which is provided for the purpose.

The Bolt – Must be kept free from oil, and must be the correct one for the rifle, *ie*, must carry the same number as that shown on the hood and on the sight leaf.

Gas escapes – Must be kept free from oil and dirt.

General

The rifle is issued specially as a sniping rifle, and although a bayonet is issued with it, it should not be used for bayonet fighting practice. The woodwork of the rifle must on no account be cut down, and as, when it is issued, it is correctly zeroed to suit one man's hold, it should not be transferred to another man without rezeroing it to suit *his* particular hold.

Related titles published by Helion & Company

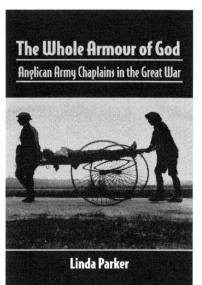

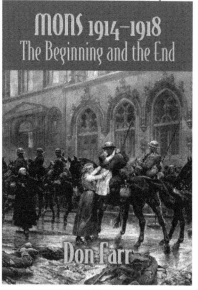

The Whole Armour of God:
Anglican Army Chaplains in the
Great War
Linda Parker
96pp   Paperback
ISBN 978-1-906033-42-2

Mons 1914–1918:
The Beginning and the End
Don Farr
256pp   Hardback
ISBN 978-1-906033-28-6

A selection of forthcoming titles

Landrecies to Cambrai. Case studies of German offensive and defensive operations
on the Western Front 1914–17
Duncan Rogers (ed.)   ISBN 978-1-906033-76-7

The Other Side of the Wire Volume 1:
With the German XIV Reserve Corps on the Somme, September 1914–June 1916
Ralph J. Whitehead   ISBN 978-1-906033-29-3

The Silent General – Horne of the First Army.
A Biography of Haig's Trusted Great War Comrade-in-Arms
Don Farr   ISBN 978-1-906033-47-7

HELION & COMPANY
26 Willow Road, Solihull, West Midlands, B91 1UE, England
Tel 0121 705 3393   Fax 0121 711 4075
Website: http://www.helion.co.uk